Awesom

and

Exciting Experiences

Travel Articles by Robert M Weir

Published in *Encore* Magazine, 1996 to 2023

Published and printed by Kindle Direct Publishing
under the auspices of Robert M. Weir and
Press On Publishing, Kalamazoo, Michigan, USA

ISBN (assigned by Kindle Direct Publishing):
9798396412415

Distributed in print-on-demand paperback and
as an eBook on Amazon.com

Unless otherwise indicated, all photos are courtesy of *Encore Magazine* or provided by the subjects of the articles

All issues of *Encore Magazine,* from the beginning through the present, are archived and available for viewing in the History Room at the Kalamazoo Public Library

The graphic at the top of the next page is the early *Encore* logo

Most photos, unless otherwise credited, were taken by Robert M Weir.

***encore:* (noun)**
a return to center stage,
to the spotlight,
one more time
amidst uproarious applause

Dedicated to the readers of *Encore Magazine* and the people whose stories grace the pages of this book

Special acknowledgements and gratitude to Phil Schubert, Penny and Rick Briscoe, Marie and Krieg Lee, and the staff at *Encore*

About the Cover

The images on the cover of *Awesome Adventures and Exciting Experiences* are photos taken by or of the author during his domestic and international travels:

- His Holiness, the Dalai Lama
- Robert Weir on the Leh-Manli Highway in the Himalaya Mountains
- The Russian tall ship *Mir* sailing at sunset on the Black Sea during the Historical Seas Tall Ship Regatta
- Robert Weir in the General Assembly of the United Nations
- The prow and bowsprit of the schooner *America*
- Robert Weir with a Tibetan elder in Leh, India
- Robert Weir with children in a non-traditional school in the slums of Kolkata (Calcutta), India
- Back cover: Robert Weir at the helm of the schooner *Pride of Baltimore II*

Awesome Adventures and Exciting Experiences

Contents

The Beginning and The Ongoing

The Author's Journeys

Tales gleaned from Robert Weir's singular assignments to distant states, the high seas, and faraway lands

Foreword by Penny Briscoe

It was always a pleasure to receive across my editor's desk a story newly written by Robert Weir. He captures the heart of his subjects, whether a person or place. He turns an experience into an adventure for his readers. His precision and attention to detail is a gift on which he has thankfully capitalized.

I have known Robert for most of my adult life. We met at a small local high school when he worked for a yearbook publishing company and I was the school's yearbook advisor. I saw then that he had a knack for publishing as he successfully and gently guided my students—and inexperienced me—to successful publications that reflected the personality and activities of the high school.

As our lives unfolded, he left to become a freelance writer and I left teaching for magazine publishing. We, sadly for several years, lost touch, what with our life changes.

Then, many years later, having just bought Encore Publishing Company, I needed writers I could trust. Bob and I had a fortuitous meeting one late evening in a local grocery store. I learned that he would happy to write feature stories for me. It was the beginning of a new and wonderful professional relationship that lasted 14 years—until my husband, Rick, and I sold the business and I moved on again to a new life.

By this time, my professional relationship with Bob had become a solid friendship, and we continued with a more purposely cemented relationship, sharing many life philosophies and passions. And it is through this tried-and-true friendship that I write this Foreword to endorse Bob's work with *Encore.*

I am a traveler who likes to relish the world personally or through reading, so Bob's ability to spin an inspiring travel tale from his own experiences was a particularly welcome attraction for *Encore Magazine.* Of special note are his unique sailing stories that reflect his knowledge of the sport and love for the open water. The experiences brought the *Encore* readership closer to such intangible adventures themselves.

Bob has a gift for telling people's life stories. One of his stories in particular brought tears to my eyes as he told about a dog named Odie and his love and dedication for his owner who needed a competent, caring service dog. Odie told his own beautiful story through words given to him by Bob, and in so doing captured this loving pup's affection for his owner.

A companion story gave Odie's human friend his own voice in expressing his appreciation for such a valuable dog friend. I truly hope Bob includes it amongst his collection of *Encore* stories in this publication of his work for *Encore.* (Author's Note: The story of photographer Marc Kelemen and his service dog, Odie, is the first story I wrote for *Encore*; it is the lead story in this book.)

Bob's breadth of topics has been another asset and strength for him as a writer. As an example, he has demonstrated the ability to accurately and effectively write about the arts and people involved in the arts. One year, when the local symphony was searching for a new conductor, he wrote a series of vignettes each time a guest conductor was scheduled to perform. His work was concise and interesting and helped the readership get to know those who crossed the performance stage. Such storytelling added to the local history of events and people and archived an artistic touch of class to the community.

Robert Weir's feature-story volume represents a lovely cross-section of Southwest Michigan, some of travel, some of the arts, some of lives in the area and how they have touched others. In many ways, Bob's collection compares to a local print version of the National Story Caravan initiative.

Telling stories has, throughout history, been important for families, communities, and humanity in general. *Encore Magazine*'s motto during my editorship was, "Every Life Has a Story." That is a universally true statement, but, unfortunately, not every story is told.

Robert Weir has brought many, many people's lives to the forefront through his writing, and I hope you enjoy the features he has captured.

Foreword by Marie Lee

When I and my husband, Krieg, bought *Encore* in 2011, Bob Weir was not listed as an asset of the sale, but he should have been. Despite some of the changes we made, such as an emphasis on shorter feature stories, Bob stuck with *Encore* and continued to give us great articles and writing.

Through Bob's stories, our readers have met inspiring people, learned about important topics, and lived a bit vicariously through Bob's adventures. When he took his nomadic sabbatical from 2018-2022, I would often be asked, "Where's Bob Weir? Why doesn't Bob write for *Encore* anymore?"

I realized then that Robert M. Weir was more than just a byline to our readers, they knew him for his interesting, informative, and warm writing. Readers looked upon him as a standard part of the magazine, like a regular feature they looked forward to each month.

When Bob told me he wanted to compile his decades of writing for *Encore* into a book, I gave him my full blessing with appreciation for its synchronous release with *Encore*'s 50th anniversary.

Bob's stories give readers a snapshot of the community this magazine has celebrated for half a century. There is no other writer for *Encore* who has done so much for so long and so well.

Whether, though this book, you are revisiting articles you've read before or reading them for the first time, you will undoubtedly find Bob's storytelling relevant, refreshing, and worthwhile.

Introduction by Robert M Weir

This book, *Awesome Adventures and Exciting Experiences*, is a companion piece to another of my books, *Outstanding People and their Amazing Accomplishments.* Both consist of a compilation of articles that I wrote for *Encore Magazine* in Kalamazoo, Michigan, from October 1996 to the summer of 2023.

Outstanding People and their Amazing Accomplishments contains 134 articles and 41 sidebars/ stories about, well, outstanding people who I am honored and privileged to have met through these assignments for *Encore.*

In contrast, *Awesome Adventures and Exciting Experiences* contains 33 articles or sidebars about my travels—domestic and international—that *Encore* chose to publish. These focus on my journeys and my unusual way of traveling to unique places and the "travel angels" who helped me have exciting experiences there.

Robert Weir sits with copies of *Encore Magazine* that contain articles he authored. He is holding the February 2105 issue that featured his experiences at the Detroit Tigers spring training camp in Lakeland, Fla., in 2014. Other visible issues have his cover features about the Civil Rights Movement, retreat centers in Southwest Michigan, the Kalamazoo Valley Blues Association, Hether Frayer as the Fresh Food Fairy, and the Kalamazoo Public Safety's K-9 Division. Photo by Brian Powers

My purpose in presenting this book is to inspire you to step out of your comfort zone, travel to usual and unusual places, and experience the foods, music, and culture of people in other parts of the world.

Gurus tell us to live in the moment. Yet, we humans inherently cling to our memories, our recollections. Our stories.

Stories are the myths and dreams, the legends and legacies, the brick and mortar of human experience.

Adversity stories. Accomplishment stories. Adventure stories. Stories of experiences. The odysseys of heroes. The lore of heroines.

The stories compiled in this book exemplify the maxim: "A journey of a thousand miles begins with a single step." It illustrates the Field of Dreams concept: "Build it and they will come."

When Phil Schubert published the stories in the first *Encore* magazine in September 1973, did he imagine that his creation—his "baby"—would, in fifty years, grow into an informational institution in Southwest Michigan?

Certainly, he must have had faith in his endeavor; after all, he birthed *Encore* and took the chance that it would be accepted by the Kalamazoo community.

Eighteen years later, in 1991, Schubert published a special collectors edition of 39 key articles about some of the principal movers and shakers in the Greater Kalamazoo area.

In that book, *The Best of Encore Magazine,* he penned these thematic words, which are both a tribute to *Encore* and the people and community about which and for which the magazine is published:

"Deeply rooted in the factors that make a community a great place to live are its people. Their character, their leadership, their perspectives, their humanity —and, yes, even their senses of humor— all contribute mightily to a community's quality and its continuing evolution in a positive direction."

So, yes, I think we can say that Schubert believed in *Encore* and its potential for longevity.

We can ask the same "Did they know …" question of the owners/publishers/editors who followed in Schubert's footsteps: Penny and Rick Briscoe then Marie and Krieg Lee.

The Briscoes owned *Encore* from 1996 to 2010, so they nurtured the publication through its 25th anniversary. I recall Penny wondering about a 50th anniversary year even back then.

The Lees are the current owners. They have the most recent view, and they are well aware of the significance of this golden anniversary of a magazine that, in this era of electronic media, continues to be a printed and online pillar of culture, people, and trends in this part of the state.

Likewise, we can ask: Did the *people* featured in *Encore* over the years and decades realize they were contributing to the ever-expanding energy that *is Encore?* The *essence* of *Encore?* The answers for them, more than likely, are as diverse as the subjects themselves.

What is there about taking that initial step of putting something into motion that stimulates the human body/mind/spirit to move forward and manifest that something into magnificence?

My answer, in a word, is *momentum.* Momentum is sneaky. It starts and incubates from that initial "first step."

When I wrote those early people articles for *Encore* in 1996—on a Mac II—I had no idea that I would be sitting at a sleek laptop 27 years later compiling a summary of those articles into *Outstanding People and their Amazing Accomplishments.*

Nor did I have a clue that I would begin to travel extensively a few years later. I didn't envision that Penny and then Marie would afford to me the special privilege of writing and submitting travel articles.

It naturally follows that I also had no idea way back then I would, one day, be presenting my travel stories in *Amazing Adventures and Exciting Experiences.*

Here in *Encore*'s 50th year, I am honored to contribute to the magazine's heritage by bringing these articles about people and about adventures to life and, once again, offering them into your awareness.

I thank God for implanting within my psyche the inclination that motivated me to carefully dissect the cover and my articles out of each issue, put those tear sheets into plastic sheet protectors and three-ring binders, and keep them.

Looking back now, I see those early articles are the seed for these two related books.

In its fifty years, *Encore* has published over 500 individual issues: nine per year at first then eventually monthly. In that half century, thousands of persons and entities have graced its pages.

Readers locally and in other states, if not abroad, have learned about the people, happenings, trends, organizations, and institutions that make this part of the world great, thrilling, and culturally profound. And, once in a while, they had an opportunity to read one of my adventure stories too.

Our human world exists through stories. Thank you for reading mine. I hope you will shout yours from the rooftops.

Stepping Back in Time Aboard Schooner *America*

From the wheel, the. great ship lays a hundred feet before me, the tip of the bow sprit 34 feet beyond that. She's 25 feet wide at the beam. An expansive sea of teak moving gently through Lake Huron on her way to Mackinac Island, a guest ship in the annual Port Huron-Mackinac sailboat race.

Ahead, the water is dark, slightly darker than the night sky, which, above, is illuminated by a myriad of stars and ghost grays of the Milky Way. The Big Dipper, the Drinking Gourd, tilts next to the aft shroud on the port side. That celestial formation is one of five directional guides to which I, at the helm of this beautiful vessel, refer during this night watch. White numbers on the black compass inside a hooded brass binnacle are illuminated by a soft red light that doesn't disturb my night vision. 340 degrees. Steady as she goes. A fluxgate compass, resettable to show the ship's position in relation to the desired course, is at zero, the center point. "Good," the captain says. He's a man of few words.

I seldom look at these three guides, the dipper and the two compasses. Rather, my hands, gripping the macramé Hawk's Head cordage on the varnished teak wheel, feel the steady pulse of water gliding past the tiller. A good feeling. My eyes follow the lights on the far forward horizon: a buoy, six miles ahead, that flashes green every four seconds and, beyond that, five mercury vapor lights—five that will become many—on Middle Island. Five lights that glow at the point where dark sky meets dark water. "Steady as she goes" means keeping the lights centered between the ship's masts and the forward port shroud. If they touch the shroud, I'm steering too far starboard; if they disappear in front of the masts, I'm off course to port. Check the compass. Sure enough, off by five degrees. "Hold her steady," the captain says. Bring her back easy, I tell myself. Bring her back easy.

I had learned during my first watch, my first attempt at the wheel, 12 hours earlier, that it's easy to oversteer. Turning the wheel and holding it until the bow is pointed in the proper direction results in the ship crossing that point and swinging to the opposite side. Even if the captain doesn't see the errancy, his experience feels it, and he can look astern and see the S-curve wake that lingers on the lake's surface for 300 yards behind us. With his elbow firm at his side, he, on that earlier watch, would raise his hand level with his chest and point with a single finger to the desired direction; the movement was subtle, a firm but gentle directive intended only for me, at the wheel, to see—not for the other passengers, or even Drew, my watch mate. I oversteered often during that first watch, and the compass followed, swinging ten degrees or more from side to side. I left a large S wake.

But I can't let my hands and inexperience take all the blame for such tortuosity. My mind wandered, too. I was enraptured with the ship.

Schooner *America* was built in 1995. She's a replica—except for the diesel engines, galley, passenger salons, and keel—of the original *America,* which was built in 1851 by members of the New York Yacht Club in response to a racing challenge from Britain's Royal Yacht Squadron. This *America* is the modern version of the boat that soundly defeated fourteen of Britain's finest sailing yachts in a 51-mile race around the Isle of Wight and after which the famous America's Cup race is named.

The hull is cedar, painted lustrous black, and adorned with large gold nameplates. The masts are Douglas fir. The booms, white oak. The deck, natural sun-bleached teak, pale like the skin of a Victorian virgin. The cabin covers are also teak, varnished to the color of lightly creamed coffee. From top to bottom, from stem to stern, *America* shines, polished, scrubbed, and swabbed. She's the biggest and steadiest boat I've ever been privileged to sail.

As we set sail from Port Huron the day before, I couldn't help but appreciate the strength and skill of the original sailors, men of courage born prior to the Civil War. It took seven of us to hoist the sails on this modern schooner, three on the gaff halyard and four on the sail halyards, all pulling simultaneously. And there were four sails—mainsail, staysail, foresail, and Yankee jib. Six thousand square feet of cloth. The mainsail and staysail more than 1,500 pounds each. Each halyard was over 200 feet long—enough rope to outfit 20 swings on a school playground—and they came down three feet at a time as the sail's leathered-covered hoops slid smoothly, but slowly, up the 108-foot masts.

This photo shows *America*'s bow, part of the bow sprit, and the loosely knit "safety net" that extends forward from the prow. Sarnia, Ontario, is in the distant background. I took this photo while standing on the net next to the bowsprit.

Jesse, 17 years old and one of *America*'s regular crew, jumped the halyard, heaving it down onto the winch. I was the first tailer, responsible for avoiding overrides. Drew and Rob tailed behind me.

Now, I'm in decent shape, by modern standards. 5'10". 150 pounds. I swim, run, and sail. But pulling on those halyards, I was well aware that most of my days are spent tapping fingertips on a keyboard. Not sufficient exercise for intense exertion. With the mainsail a little more than half way up, I began to huff Lamaze style and time inhalations with each pull. The others were doing the same while Jesse, with his youthful lungs also huffing, called the cadence. "Pull. Pull. Pull." I wanted to look up—how much more?—but I didn't dare. My job is to make sure the halyard doesn't override, so my eyes remained on the halyard, wrapped three times around the winch, watching it come off the outer side as Jesse's pulls brought more and more, always more, halyard down onto the inner side. My arms ached. Triceps and forearm muscles screamed with internal heat. Finally, Jesse stopped.

"Why you stop?" The voice was Pedro's, the Italian first mate, probably the strongest person onboard.

"Got to rest." Jesse said. Thank you, Jesse. My chest heaved as I held firm on the halyard. Perspiration dripped from my brow. But the reprieve lasted—what?—no more than four seconds. Then we hauled the halyard again, finishing the task with another twenty heaves.

Imagine the same event 150 years ago. Races, then, started with ships at anchor (unlike today's races that begin with boats on the move and sailors counting down the seconds, aiming for a precision start). Hoisting sails and raising the anchor in the days of the original *America* were part of the race. The sails were true canvas, not cotton Dacron. And there were no mechanical winch motors to raise the anchor.

These thoughts come flooding back as I hold the wheel steady on my night watch. Good seamen, they must have been. The muscles in their legs and arms and backs honed by constant exertion, constantly remaining steady on a constantly moving, sometimes heaving, deck. Muscles honed by frequent strenuous activity.

Even while under way, there were things to do, for this ship is home to Captain Zimmerman, Pedro, Jesse, Kate, Christine, and Abbey. Like any home, it requires maintenance.

Prior to our departure, Pedro and Jesse had spliced and sewn new 3/4" lines for the lazy jacks on the staysail; the task had taken several hours. Then, we had hoisted Jesse up, in the boatswain's chair, to the top of the masts to rerun the new jacks through a wooden block.

The night, as I stand my watch, is full of sounds. Above me, a strap on the mainsail boom creaks a steady uuuhhrrr, uuuhhrrr, uuuhhrrr as we rock in gentle waves that are fueled by a ten-knot breeze. Water cavitating behind the stern thrums like spring water tumbling over logs in a mountain brook, but this boat is the log, moving through lake water at five knots. Fast for a smaller boat, like the 30- to 40-footers I normally sail on. But five knots on the *America* is like being in a baby carriage. And even the rising moon, which casts a shimmering glow across rippling water, shines on the starboard quarter and seems to coo like a mother singing softly to her northbound child.

The green beacon, closer than the

Robert Weir stands at the helm of *America*, his hands on the Hawk's Head knotting that provides a tactile sensation for proper steering. Watch mate Drew is in the background. Lower right: Robert hauls on a line to help the crew lower a sail.

mercury vapors, now passes beside us to our port. I look at my watch. It's taken us an hour to sail six miles — fast by sailing standards, which seems to displace land time with a patient primal reality foreign to stop signs and concrete. The depth meter says we're still in 40 feet of water. "Good," the captain says. And I do feel good. I've learned to steer. When I stray, let's say, to starboard, I now, almost unconsciously, turn the wheel to port — "Just like steering a car," Drew tells me.

But it's not like steering a car. This is a fluid environment where things happen as they happen, when they happen. And a ship this big is slow to respond. Fifteen or twenty seconds after turning the wheel, the rudder is finally affected by water passing on both sides of it. Only then, does the ship begin to correct its course. Only then, do I see the long bow sprit and the darkened foredeck begin to swing slowly back to port and the lights on Middle Island come back into their proper relational position with the boat. But before they do, before we're headed in the right direction, I turn the wheel back to starboard. The ship continues to swing to port for another fifteen or twenty seconds, continuing to move in the opposite direction of this most recent turn of the wheel. Then, the great ship settles in. The lights are centered, again, between the port shrouds and the masts. The fluxgate compass rests at zero. 340 degrees on the conventional compass. "Good," says the captain.

The next day, steering off course even two degrees is not good. Zero, dead on, is the only allowable direction. The reason is that on this new day, as Drew and I take our morning watch, we are within sight of Mackinac Island, dead ahead to the northwest. The wind is blowing out of the west-southwest, so we're close hauled on a port tack.

The weather forecast is predicting thunderstorms and shifting winds that will soon blow straight off the island, toward us. Under sail power, boats don't go straight into the wind, and the captain wants to make land—make the finish line—before the wind shifts and we're forced to tack our way in. "Let her ride up (into the wind) on the puffs," he tells me, "then bring her back to zero."

We're traveling at 10 knots, drawn through the water by winds blowing 20 to 25. Still *America* is steady. So is my greater, constant pressure on the wheel, for this boat has a weather helm, and she definitely wants to ride to windward. The captain's instructions mean that I can ease my tense muscles a little, but not too much, in the puffs and let the ship head where she naturally wants to go, but then I have to pull the wheel back in the lulls. Drew and I take 20 minute turns. This is not easy work.

Close to Mackinac Island and moving fast toward rocks on the west breakwall, I ask the captain if he wants to take the wheel. Surprised, I hear him say, "No. When you hear the (finish)

Crewmember Kate Lynch takes her turn at the wheel as the sun rises on Lake Huron. Kate has lived aboard schooner *America* for three years, having sailed the ship twice across the Atlantic and along the Eastern Seaboard from the Caribbean to New York.

gun, turn her into the wind and we'll drop the sails."

And that's what we do. I hold course. We hear the gun. I turn to windward. And we drop the sails. They come down easier than they went up. But there's still the scramble, the organized rush as the crew brings those big, heavy sails and gaff rigging down the masts and ties them with reefing hitches to the booms.

Then, there is quiet. Oh, the twin 220 horse diesels are chugging now. But the feeling, the motion, of being powered through the water under raised sail is gone. Land is at hand. And the thrill of a lifetime will soon be over.

The Au Sable, the Grand:
River Expeditions Reveal History and Change

The Au Sable. The Grand. Two Michigan rivers. Both named by French explorers: The Au Sable for its sand*; The Grand for its great length.

* French explorers may have named the Au Sable River because of sand at its mouth—rare on Michigan's stony east shore—or after a tribe of Ottawa Indians who lived along the river and whom the French also called Au Sable or "people of the sand." Some historians also note an early minor French explorer who was named Sable.

Jim Miller paddles his birchbark canoe through quiet waters and early morning mist on the Au Sable River near Rollways scenic overlook. In front of Miller is a split ash basket that he also made; behind him is a buffalo robe that was his bed during a six-day voyage down the entire length of the Au Sable. Miller carved his paddle from basswood. He used a knife to etch images of beaver and moose into the prow of his canoe. The lacing is made from spruce roots, and the curved wood atop the gunwale is cedar. Photos by Robert M Weir

The Au Sable, combined with the Manistee River, forms a navigable inland water route from Oscoda on Lake Huron to the city of Manistee on Lake Michigan; half the distance in either direction, is, of course, upstream, with the peninsular divide at a portageable marsh near Grayling.

The Grand is the longest river in the state, flowing from headwaters west of Lake LeAnn in northeast Hillsdale County to its mouth in Grand Haven, with the last few miles being a bayou.

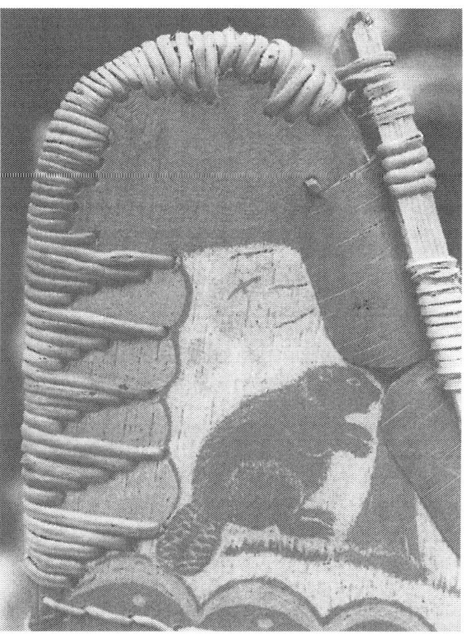

These French and Indian connections came to life for me last May and July on extensive canoe trips on both rivers.

The Au Sable trip originated with Jim Miller who lives within the Huron National Forest and not far from Oscoda and Lake Huron. Jim travels to schools in Michigan, Colorado, and Alaska, teaching Native American and aboriginal skills. His demonstrations include making fire from friction, brain-tanning hides, flintknapping arrow heads and knives, constructing baskets from ash splits or birchbark, and building protective shelters from native woody materials and woven cattail mats. While constructing his birchbark canoe, Jim asked if I would join him for its maiden voyage on the Au Sable. Yes, indeed!

We started from Grayling, 20 miles downstream from the headwaters, on a cool, cloudy May 8. There were three of us in the party: Jim in his birchbark, and Ben Kent and myself in—dare I say—my aluminum canoe.

While Jim portrayed his Native American persona, Ben provided the French connection with a voyageur song he taught us and which we sang while rhythmically dipping our paddles into the water.

Vent frais, vent du matin,
Vent qui soufl' aux sommets des grands pins,
Joie du vent qui soufl',
Allons dans le grand vent.

The translation is:

Fresh wind, wind of the morning,
Wind that blows in the tops of the tall pines,
How wonderful is the wind that blows,
Let's go into the strong wind.

Go into the strong wind, we did. For much of six days and 120 miles, the wind blew at more than 10 miles per hour. Crossing the backwater of Loud Dam, we encountered whitecaps high enough to splash over our bow as we cut through them. Especially in those conditions, Ben and I had it easy in comparison to Jim, who, alone in his canoe, had to stroke twice as fast to match our tandem efforts.

At other times, usually in early morning or where tree-lined banks protected us from the wind, we cruised along at a gentle pace, enjoying stories and song and serenity that can only be realized when modern transportation is miles away, tucked into a parking lot, out of sight and sound and mind for several days.

Ben's father is Tim Kent of Silver Fox Enterprises and a retired Chicago Symphony trumpeter and Michigan historian. After the trip, he reminded us of how much the Au Sable has changed since the 1600s, the era of French explorers Samuel Champlain, Etienne Brule, Jean Pere, Adrien Joliet, and Robert Cavalier de La Salle.

The dams are one big difference—five of them that seem to have been built for their present-day purpose of manufacturing hydroelectricity. In actuality, the dams were constructed to augment Michigan's lumber industry in the early 1800s. "There were thousands of logs floated down the Au Sable to sawmills and ships on Lake Huron," Kent said. "They put in dams to control water depths. Instead of a major torrent of water flowing for a few days, they could have a manageable flow for a number of weeks."

Kent commented on vast number of acres the lumbering industry denuded within the Au Sable watershed and soil erosion at high banks and rollways where logs were spilled into the river. The natural beauty, pretty much void of houses, that we saw in 2000 is a testimony to Earth's ability to heal and restore itself—if we, humankind, leave it alone.

A more insidious change has resulted from attempts to dry out Michigan's lowlands and wetlands with drainage systems. Kent said that, at the time of French explorers and Native American Indians before them, the waters of the Au Sable flowed more freely and more slowly. Except during spring thaws and heavy rains, the current would allow strong paddlers, those who used waterways as highways, to move upstream at a rate of three miles per hour. Paddling against the current in craft that preceded today's sleek styles and featherweight materials was hard work, but the alternative of carrying hundreds of pounds of supplies or pelts overland was far, far inferior.

As Jim, Ben, and I paddled or drifted from Grayling to Oscoda and out onto Lake Huron, we saw numerous pike, trout, salmon and—I swear—a shimmering silver sturgeon, half the length of our canoe, that was steady in a deep pool one moment and gone in a flash the next.

Beaver lodges were huge, and fallen trees on which the beaver dined, numerous. Best of all, we saw four bald eagles. In contrast, we observed only three airplanes, all on our last day as we neared Oscoda. There, too, we heard lawn mowers for the first time on our journey; their noise was blasphemous.

I experienced another contrast in mid-July on the Grand, a southern Michigan river that has been adversely affected by much greater human population and development. For example, in contrast to the Au Sable being a host environment for bald eagles, the Grand River flows through three cities—Jackson, Lansing, and Grand Rapids—that sport international airports.

My trip on the Grand was part of the Grand River Expedition 2000. In 1990 and again last summer, a flotilla of nearly 120 men, women, boys, and girls paddled 225 miles in 12 days from Michigan Center, south of Jackson, to Lake Michigan. In nine cities along the way, they set up interpretive displays to inform and educate people about the condition of the major waterway that flows through and connects their communities.

John Slawinski, an environmental outreach coordinator for General Motors, canoed and fished the entire length on both expeditions. He took daily water samples and made chemical tests, approved by the U.S. Environmental Protection Agency, for dissolved oxygen levels and other water quality indicators. Slawinski reported the river is in better condition than ten years ago, primarily because of clean-up efforts and increased public appreciation for this resource. He and other trip organizers credited municipalities for separating storm water runoff systems from sewers that carry human and household waste.

But Slawinski also noted human encroachment. Erosion and exposed tree roots from flash flooding, which is the result of draining wetlands for agricultural or residential purposes, were common in narrow sections; drainage pipes of various dimensions fed into the river in many locations. Erosion was prevalent at home sites where residents mowed their yards—or worse, planted and manicured non-native, short-rooted Kentucky blue grass—right to the river's edge rather than allowing a natural setback of indigenous, deep-rooted, soil-retaining vegetation. Algae-forming phosphates and nutrients were highly concentrated in areas where fertilizers had been flushed by rainwater from farms and lawns. Cattle, one source of deadly e-coli contamination, were seen wading in the river.

For the Grand River Expedition 2000, I showed up in Ada, Michigan, alone with my 16-foot aluminum canoe. After seeing me struggle to keep up with paddlers in lightweight kayaks, an expedition organizer suggested that I park my canoe on one of the transport trailers and, for the remaining five days of the voyage, become an oarsman on the French *bateau Squateck*. In this photo, I'm the person behind and closest to the sail—not rowing but adjusting the sail to catch a following breeze. Photo by Ron St. Germaine

A leak from a ruptured fuel supply line not only drove up gas prices in Michigan last summer, but also necessitated sausage-shaped floating retention booms to prevent gasoline from washing downstream from where that leak, in Ingham County, flowed into the Grand River. The Michigan Department of Environmental Quality reported that 75,000 gallons of fuel spilled into the waterway; most of that, 60,000 gallons, was retained by the booms and vacuumed into tank trucks, but 15,000 gallons breached the booms during a rainstorm.

Karen Betten, the expedition's secretary, said a person from the Ingham County Department of Environmental Health said that, on the day of the leak, gas two feet deep floated atop the water and fish were jumping through it to get air. The retention booms were still in place when the expedition paddlers came through, and they saw dead fish and turtles.

Slawinski mixed these reports with comments about "miles and miles of beautiful spots" that reminded him of up-north, even Canadian, rivers. In places of lesser urban development, where tree canopies shaded and cooled the water, he found macroinvertebrates and bugs, like caddisflies and gilled snails, on which fish feed. In these areas, the fishing was good. He noted that mosquito-eating swallows build nests on horizontal ledges under bridges and suggested working this feature into bridge design. As an icon of nature's ability to, sometimes, adapt around the human species, Slawinski noted a bald eagle's nest atop the crossbar of a telephone pole.

I joined the expedition in Ada, upstream from Grand Rapids. My aluminum canoe soon proved to be too cumbersome for a lone paddler in the slow, wide waters there. Fortunately, my solo situation was also my ticket to a grand adventure with another Indian and French connection.

Within sight of the foot dams that are the concrete version of what were once the Grand River's "grand rapids," Jim Ledford, wearing French reenactment apparel, offered me a deal: he would paddle with me in my aluminum canoe through the city's shallow waters and portages in exchange for me joining him, and others, later in *Gabagouache*, a 26-foot replica of a birchbark canoe, that, because of its size and weight, was going to be transported on a trailer around the city. My answer was as quick and affirmative as it was to Jim Miller's invitation about the Au Sable trip.

Once through Grand Rapids, I and a dozen or more people launched *Gabagouache* and her companion vessel *Squateck*, a wooden French *bateau*. Then I put my canoe on the trailer used to carry these two craft and didn't see it again for another four days, until after our arrival in Grand Haven.

Dave Seibold, a historian with the Tri-Cities Museum in Grand Haven, sat in the stern and steered *Gabagouache* as he spoke from under a tall black top hat and from behind a felt beard. He told his passengers that *gabagouache* is an Anishinaabe Indian word, meaning "big mouth," used by native peoples to describe the Grand River's wide expanse where it flowed into Lake Michigan; this was, of course, before its waters were constricted to a present-day, concrete-and-steel channel.

The museum commissioned construction of *Gabagouache* for the Grand Haven sesquicentennial in 1984. It can carry 15 passengers and 1.5 tons of cargo. This size is appropriate for its purpose of helping people, especially youngsters, experience early Native American river travel. Yet, the working canoes of three to five centuries ago, after which *Gabagouache* is patterned, were 35 to 40 feet long and could carry nearly double that cargo. Those canoes were so wide that non-rowing passengers in the center of the boat sat four abreast on narrow wooden benches.

Research historian and author Janie Lynn Panagopoulos of Rockford, Illinois, was also aboard *Gabagouache*. She said she had seen a globe in Venice, dated 1681, that shows La Grande Riviere in quite accurate detail.

Panagopoulos, who wore a long European dress and wide-brimmed hat with a white feather typical of the 1700s, explained that Robert Cavalier de La Salle found himself stranded at present day St. Joseph, Michigan, when his ship, the *Griffen*, the first European ship on the Great Lakes, was lost on Lake Michigan. Historians believe the ship was loaded beyond its limits with illegally trapped furs when it sailed from Mackinac for Wisconsin. La Salle, himself, was not aboard the vessel; rather, he and a band of his men canoed from the straits along the west Michigan shore.

The *Griffen* was to meet La Salle and his men in southern Lake Michigan, but when the appointed time of rendezvous came and went, they canoed back up the coast, first looking for the lost ship, then, for a shortcut to Detroit. Seeing promise in the wide mouth of the Grand, La Salle left his men and walked eastward, following the river to its headwaters, then orienteered across the remainder of Michigan's lower peninsula. Within months, the explorer was back in France, and Panagopoulos credits La Salle with the accurate mapping of La Grande Riviere on the 1681 globe.

Research historian and author Janie Lynn Panagopoulos poses with Kosta and Alec Karis of Muskegon next to the birchbark replica canoe *Gabagouache*. The three are dressed in European clothing of the 1700s. When not held up, the dress would cover a woman's ankles, but raising the hem to keep the material dry was a common practice when getting in or out of such a canoe. Men, who were accustomed to getting their legs wet on such a journey, often wore buckskin leggings or, if no women were on board, only a loin cloth.

The next morning, while camped next to a football field at Grand Valley State University, I received an invitation from Jim Meyerle, director of Project Lakewell, a nonprofit organization in Lansing that promotes education about the Great Lakes and its tributaries, to join his crew in *Squateck*.

This double-ended, 600-pound, 24.5-foot wooden *bateau* is a replica of the first European-style boats to enter the Great Lakes in the mid-1600s; the original vessels were 35 to 40 feet in length and could carry more than two tons of cargo.

Squateck's name comes from the Mic-Mac Indian language and means "division of the waters," in reference to a high point of land, a "divide," that separates watersheds. Serving as an example, a town of Squatteck (with two ts) lies on Notre Dame peninsula in Quebec province; near there, at the divide of the northern Appalachian Range, mountain water flows north and west toward the Saint Laurent Riviere as well as east toward Chaleur Bay and the Gulf of Saint Lawrence.

Meyerle wanted me on board because he had heard I was a sailor, the weather forecast called for a strong southerly wind that morning, the Grand River flows due north for several miles, and—joy of joys—*Squateck* is equipped with a square canvas sail that had not yet been raised on this expedition.

For those initial miles, we easily and lazily kept pace with canoes and kayaks that were propelled by pairs of arms and paddles. To them and for ourselves, we raised our voices in lusty song:

> What do you do with a drunken voyageur?
> What do you do with a drunken voyageur?
> What do you do with a drunken voyageur?
> Earl-lie in the morning?

And the famed reprise:

> Shave his belly with a rusty razor.
> Shave his belly with a rusty razor.
> Shave his belly with a rusty razor.
> Earl-lie in the morning.

As was the tradition of French voyageurs, we made up additional verses as we went, and Meyerle related fur trade stories as he, the *gouverner* or person who governs the *gouvernail* (rudder or helm), steered us carefully down the river.

Reveille on Day 13, the expedition's last day, at Ottawa County's Riverside Park was, per usual, at six o'clock. Group breakfast of cereal, fruit, juice, and yogurt was served at 6:30. The daily briefing by our river master, 77-year-old world-renowned paddler Verlen Kruger, included information about navigating the bayou, how to find our scheduled lunch stop, and what to expect if the Coast Guard, indeed, allowed us to paddle all the way through Grand Haven and onto Lake Michigan.

Unfortunately, the wind had shifted over night and was now blowing hard from the west, opposite to our desired direction. Because of *Squateck*'s heavy weight and lack of sleekness, we hit the water early, prior to 7:30.

We had eight on board: Jim Meyerle, the *gouverner;* Brandon Lehrer, the *avant* who stood in the bow and kept watch for shallows or obstacles in the water; and rowers Jennifer and Julianne Meyerle (the *gouverner*'s twin daughters), Brian Reed, Robin Mersereau, Charlie Parmalee, and me.

In *Squateck,* all except the *gouverner* and the *avant* face aft; the lead rowing station is, therefore, toward the stern where the oarsmen there can be seen by the others. Reed, who fortunately was an experienced member of the Rockford High School rowing team, and I sat there and set the pace.

The current through the Grand River bayou is minimal, and, because the wind blew against us, if we stopped rowing, even for a moment, our speed quickly diminished to nothing and we would have to strain even harder to regain momentum. So, we kept going, keeping our rhythm with the cadence of our songs.

At noon and under the expedition's 12th straight day of sunshine and moderate to intense heat, we were the last vessel to approach the lunch stop, to which we were looking forward with great anticipation and hunger. Alas, as we rowed ashore, we were met by the other craft coming out.

Mike Smith, chair of the expedition's board of directors, informed us the Coast Guard had granted permission for the flotilla to pass through the channel and enter Lake Michigan, but, because of the wind and building seas, we would have to hurry. A kayaker glided alongside and handed us three bags of Arby's sandwiches. We took turns eating, two at a time, as we made our way into Grand Haven.

Abeam of the Coast Guard station near downtown and within sight of the big lake (for those who were looking forward), the swells in the channel crested at two or three feet—not much for any engine-powered craft, exciting for those in canoes and kayaks, and a special accomplishment for the troop of girl scouts who had paddled the entire length of the Grand.

For us, those waves meant we had to make a chore. I saw my oak oar, an inch-and-a-half in diameter, bend as it pivoted at the oar pin with each heave. Reed reminded us to reduce wind resistance by feathering our oars—that is, rotate them with a precise twist of the wrist so the blade cut through the wind, rather than be flat to the wind—every time we leaned forward and lifted our blades out of the water in preparation for the next stroke

Occasionally, one rower would get out of synch. At best, the loss of collective rhythm deprived us of optimum thrust; at worst, the errant oar would hit another and disrupt the *bateau*'s momentum.

The last half mile of our 14.8 miles for that day seemed to take more than an hour. It was probably less, but a solid seven hours on a wooden seat with little food and no bathroom break can make a short time seem long. This situation caused me to greatly appreciate the tenacity of early explorers and Indians who, as indicated by Tim Kent, rowed *bateaus* and paddled canoes downstream, upstream, and across the lakes' open waters for hours and days on end.

But we did make it through the channel and onto Lake Michigan. There, we rejoiced—but only for a moment, for the *gouverner* instructed us to continue rowing while he steered us straight into the waves for a distance greater than any other kayak or canoe, even *Gabagouache*, before he saw a wave pattern with which he felt we could safely turn *Squateck* around. Then, with the wind blowing from our stern, we toyed with idea of hoisting the sail, but didn't. Instead we rowed in, against the minimal current, our spirits buoyed by the way our craft surfed the swells.

We answered cheers from pedestrians on the pier with a voyageur salute: a unison double thump of oars on the gunwale, followed by lifting oar blades vertically over our heads and a shout of *"salut."*

Within another hour, we returned to a boat launch on the east side of Grand Haven. *Gabagouache* and *Squateck* were lifted out of the water and on their loft trailer, one above the other.

The Grand River Expedition officially ended with a ceremony at Waterfront Stadium in downtown Grand Haven. The mayor spoke, as did Mike Smith and Verlen Kruger. Those who had set up interpretive displays in other communities repeated their routine here.

As with any such group, especially those who had paddled the entire length of this waterway, there were deeply felt handshakes, hugs, smiles, and tears. For me and the crew of *Squateck*, there was also a lot of tired. Good tired. The kind of tired that says, Sure, I'll do it again; just give me a good meal and an hour or two to rest. Okay?

A Merry Time in Maritime England

The mammoth size of *H.M.S. Warrior*—418 feet long, 58 feet at the beam, and displacement of 9,200 tons—becomes readily apparent when she is viewed alongside other watercraft and standing among the rigging (next page). Built by the British in 1861, she was the first vessel to have an iron-plated hull and combine steam power with sail power. A docent onboard said, "*Warrior* immediately made all other warships obsolete."

On the next page, Robert Weir stands at the one of the four wheels on the helm of *Warrior*. With four wheels, it is possible for eight sailors to man the helm. Heavy ropes around the helm's drum lead through holes in the deck to another four-wheel helm on the deck below and another four-wheel helm on the deck below that. Thus, 24 sailors could stand at the helm at one time; this number was necessary during storms and battles.

On August 24 through 27, 2001, I went to southern England to attend the International Festival of the Sea (IFOS), held at Portsmouth Royal Dockyard, Portsmouth. At a cost of £4 million (nearly $6 million) to stage and with ships and boats from England, Russia, Brazil, Oman, France, Norway, Germany, Spain, The Netherlands, Poland, Italy and the United States, this was the largest maritime event in the world in 2001. This was the third IFOS; the first was held in Bristol, England, in 1992. Another is planned for 2005 in Portsmouth.

The International Festival of the Sea was a blend of romance, firepower, adventure, and exploration; a mixture of mammoth and miniature; a bonding of history and heritage; and coated with constant entertainment.

A quarter of a million people, including England's Princess Anne and husband Commodore Tim Lawrence, attended the four-day festival. Yet the crowd was not crowded in the nine-square-mile working dockyard that was also home to thousands of Royal Navy men and women.

The people there were military types in diverse uniforms, attractive lasses in fashionable English attire, ruddy recreational sailors, and people of all ages in 17th and 18th century period costume. They were teens, adults, children in strollers, and elderly, some with canes and free-for-the-asking electric carts. Whether visiting for a day or staying aboard a boat in a dockyard basin, they paid tribute to seafaring traditions of our ancestors who for millennia prior to automobiles and airplanes traveled the world's waterways by ship, boat, and canoe.

Immersed in international aromas and sunshine (three out of four days), festival visitors roamed quays, floating docks, and dry-docks looking for, and finding, maritime vistas on every horizon. They saw the Royal Air Force precision squadron, Red Arrows, fly by at low altitudes, busting the sound barrier and leaving red-dyed contrails on blue-gray skies. They heard music here, there, and everywhere—around the next building, under the next permanent overhead crane, beyond the next gray battleship, across the next wharf—bagpipers, military orchestras, rockin' combos, fife and drum corps with glockenspiels, and chantey groups with pennywhistles. Over 2,000 musicians, including the group, Hoolie, from Bay City, Michigan, performed at scheduled times on four stages, along parade routes, and impromptu in ale tents. Some minstreled on stilts. Brits are big on stilts.

Imagine the surprise on a tourist's face when, at the moment her husband presses his camera's shutter button to capture an image of her with a short, squeaky-voiced (costumed) seagull, a ten-foot peg-legged Captain Hook steps into the picture and leans his single metal digit against her cheek.

Imagine gathering around a pirate, a tar, and a blind sawbones—all on stilts—as they intone, "What do yah do with a drunken sailor?" Their question was not meant to convey song, for their banjo, abused tuba, and out-of-tune soprano sax imparted malformed melody; rather, their intent was to invite heckling, a popular form of British street humor. "Look in the bottom o' ya'r black h'arts. Thar's whar ya'll find ya'r ahnsaaar." At the end of each chorus, while his mates' plinked and ooompah-ahed, the pirate would cackle, "Ya'r an ugly lot. Look, thar's anahther one with a silver box stuck to 'is aye." Then, "What ar' ya laffin' at? No one laffs here unless I sahy soooo. Aaarrrrrrr."

Amidst all this, what to see first? Which of 1,000 ships and boats? Tall ships, Royal Navy destroyers, or the *USS Winston S. Churchill?* Great ships of British history: *Mary Rose, Victory,* and *Warrior?* Combined navy/air force/army/marine amphibian rescue demonstrations? The submarine exhibit?

Tall Ships and SeaTrek

Big masts loomed along the waterfront. Tall ships. Twenty-five of them, the largest square-riggers in the world. Among them: *Matthew*, a replica of the ship used by English explorer John Cabot, who set sail in search of Japan in 1497 and discovered Newfoundland instead; *Cisne Blanco*, built in Amsterdam for the Brazilian Navy to train cadets; *Palinuro*, an Italian navy cadet training ship; *Shtandart*, a replica of Peter the Great's 18th century warship; *Sedov*, the largest square-rigged ship in the world, built in Germany in 1921, used by Australia to haul grain, and now owned by Russia; *Astrid*, a 1918 vintage ship from Holland that may have been used for drug smuggling while under a Liberian flag in the 1970s; and *Swan Fan Makkum* of Holland, the world's largest brigantine and touted as "the ultimate in sailing luxury."

Of this venerable fleet, four ships of SeaTrek shone in the spotlight. These vessels—*Statsraad Lehmkuhl* of Germany, *Europa* of The Netherlands, and Norwegian ships *Christian Radich* and *Sorlandet*—set sail from Portsmouth on Monday, August 27, the final festival day, for a six-week passage to New York.

Their crossing marked the 150th anniversary of a voyage by 83,000 European converts to the Church of Jesus Christ of Latter Day Saints. Taking the route of those Mormons, the crew and paying passengers would follow trade winds southwest to Puerto Rico, then north to Bermuda and New York, arriving on October 4.

What would it have been like for emigrants to sail a one-way journey on tall ships to a new land in search of hope and religious freedom in the 1700 and 1800s? What would it have been like for women to leave parents behind or to carry a baby onboard? What nation would a child born at sea claim as "home," the old England or the New Land of America? What would it have been like for men of the soil to climb aloft on swaying masts to furl sails while seas roiled 150 to 200 feet below them?

A display within a Mormon-hosted tent offered an answer in the words of Englishman James Thomas Sutton, who sailed aboard *Hudson* in 1864, "We would not have turned back had we been given the chance."

Top photo: *Statsraad Lehmkuhl* under full sail. Lower photo: Two of the crew passengers rest among the ship's complex rigging.

Venerable Flagships

H.M.S. *Warrior* floats at a dock along Portsmouth Harbour. Moored nearby, 20- to 40-foot fishing boats and pleasure craft look like dwarfs. She is long, black, and sleek. Launched in 1861 to counter France's Emperor Napoleon III, *Warrior* instantly made all other warships obsolete. She was the first ship to combine sail technology with a steam engine, an iron hull, and armor plating, and she could outrun and outgun any existing battleship. In 1863, she was visited by 270,000 people on a 12-week tour around Britain.

H.M.S. Victory is the showpiece of the Portsmouth Royal Dockyard. Her height, beauty, and splendor exude beyond the massive physical space she occupies. As the flagship of Admiral Lord Nelson—famous for his motto "Never fear the event" —she imbues the spirit of British maritime pride and prominence.

Victory has as much "presence" now, even sharing this dockyard with modern warships, as she enjoyed during her extensive tour of duty. Launched in 1765, she saw the American War of Independence, the Battle of Trafalgar against Napoleon I, and proactive preservation in 1922. During her career, UI was home to at least ten captains of British Admiralty and participated in seven major nautical campaigns throughout the Atlantic and Mediterranean.

H.M.S. Mary Rose, "The Flower of all Ships," was built in Portsmouth in 1510 at the order of King Henry VIII who demanded that she be fitted with more and bigger guns than any warship had ever carried. Unfortunately, those extra cannons may have caused *Mary Rose* to capsize in a battle outside Portsmouth Harbour on July 19, 1545.

In 1982, the starboard side of the ship's hull, which had been preserved in a bed of ocean silt, was raised, towed into Portsmouth, and placed within feet of where she was built nearly 500 years earlier. These remains reside in misty repose under a spray of water-soluble wax, polyethylene glycol. This process, which began in 1994 and will take at least 15 years, will preserve the *Mary Rose*, like a flower petal pressed into a classic book, for all time.

For as fascinating and fabulous as these ships are, the story—as it always is—lies in the people. Today, visitors are welcomed aboard *Warrior* and *Victory*. Guides provide a verbal glimpse of horrendous human drama from those eras.

A guide aboard *Warrior*, after describing the ship's cannons, told his audience, "Imagine the scene here—smoke, noise, the ship was rolling, asphyxiating smoke, limbs flying everywhere. It was like a butcher shop gone wrong. Awful, awful. When the shots were fired, the ship's gunners were deafened, some of them permanently, and it was every man for himself and God for us all."

Visitors to the International Festival of the Sea stand in a long queue to walk about on *H.M.S. Victory*.

Modern Ships

Contrasted with the beauty and hand-to-hand horror of these historic vessels, the modern ships in the Portsmouth Royal Dockyard were stark gray. They possessed an image of stealth as well as a formidable physical presence. IFOS visitors queued for two hours to board guest ship *USS Winston S. Churchill*, commissioned March 2001, and other ships from Britain and Europe. Once onboard, visitors were greeted by courteous naval personnel, yet the tour was curtailed by ropes and barriers that prevented intrusion into classified areas.

H.M.S. Illustrious and *R.V. Tritan* also drew large crowds. The former, a 685-feet, 20,000 ton aircraft carrier nicknamed "Lusty," is the Royal Navy's present flagship. The latter is the world's first military trimaran and a collaboration between the United States and the United Kingdom. Ship designers believe her three hulls will provide greater stability for crew comfort, helicopter operations, and weapons firing.

Two red-hulled ships, the Royal Navy's *H.M.S. Endurance*, "The Red Plum," and privately owned *R.R.S. James Clark Ross*, were on leave from normal duties as Antarctic explorers. As was the case on England's historic flagships, interpretive guides provided interesting facts about these vessels and their crews' findings.

The *James Clark Ross* is a "world class floating laboratory" capable of moving steadily at two knots through level sea ice one meter thick. She was named after the Royal Navy Admiral and Arctic explorer who discovered the north magnetic pole in 1831.

People who work aboard are civilian employees of the British Antarctic Survey. They study the upper atmosphere, magnetic fields, water temperature, geologic and tectonic evolution, penguins and albatrosses, krill and blue whales, annual snowfall, and frozen bacteria that could be over half a million years old.

They have learned that Antarctica was once joined to South America, India, Australia, and Africa; penguins can dive to a depth of 250 meters; albatrosses with wingspans of three meters can fly up to 10,000 kilometers in 10 to 20 days; a blue whale eats four tons of krill, a zooplankton, each day; and the continent, 58 times the size of Great Britain, is technically a desert. Ice and snow there are not white, but blue, and "glisten like diamonds."

Old Gaffers and Other Wooden Boats

The Old Gaffers Association is an organization of 2,000 members throughout the British Isles, France, Germany, Scandinavia, and Australia, who are committed to preserving and promoting "the virtues of gaff- and lug -rigged [sailing] heritage." The organization originated with a race on Solent Sound, outside Portsmouth Harbour, in 1958. Only three boats showed up, yet the race became an annual event with a growing number of participants.

A similar race was held off England's east coast in 1963 and was so popular that the committees for both races joined to form the association. This year, they had a flotilla of 50 boats from throughout the British Isles, most of them wooden vessels—yawls, ketches, and cutters—many 100 years old.

Clinker-built Solent Galleys are 30-foot long rowboats with benches for four oarsmen, each pulling one oar. In concept, these wooden masterpieces are forerunners of competitive rowing skulls, but the Solent Galleys are much heavier than their chemically composited counterparts. They are primarily recreation craft today, although racers of four, five, and six decades ago would row 60 to 100 miles in races that lasted up to 12 hours.

Cornish Pilot Gigs are also rowing galleys that, with a commercial bent, raced for money in olden days. Men in gigs would row local pilots out to boats offshore so they could pilot the visiting boats in. The first gig to the inbound ship got the pilotage.

West Wight Potters are tubby wooden sailboats, no more than 15 or 16 feet in length, designed by legendary boat builder Stanley Smith on nearby Isle of Wight. They acquired their name as boats in which a sailor could "potter" around. Yet, these tiny craft also earned a reputation for tremendous seaworthiness by crossing the Atlantic Ocean and surviving gale force winds in the North Sea.

Shoal Waters is a cozy 16-foot wooden single-masted gaff-rigged boat owned by Charles and Joy Stock. Since 1963, the couple has sailed it over 68,000 miles without a motor and without accepting tows, mostly on the Thames River Estuary.

Charles, a writer, photographer, and retired farmer turned "tax man," described that area of seven rivers and multiple islands and shoals as "the best 500 square miles of sailing anywhere in the world."

The couple have accumulated their maritime miles by sailing for hours, rather than days, on end. They board *Shoal Waters* late Friday afternoon and sail with the out-going tide, sometimes at six in the evening, sometimes after midnight Saturday morning. Their pattern, nearly every weekend February through November, is to sail until the tide has nearly ebbed, then find a shoal or salt flat, lift the centerboard, drop anchor in soon-to-be-exposed mud, "brew up" some tea, and cuddle in for a few hours rest until they sense *Shoal Waters* coming afloat again.

Model Boats

For all the 1,000 boats at IFOS—historical and modern, wooden and fiberglass, sail and power, naval and private, pleasure and working craft—they were outnumbered at least five-fold by model boats. These detailed craft were made of wood, plastic, fiberglass, cloth, or whatever materials were best suited to the task. They ranged from palm size to more than human armspan. Most were on display cradles. Some floated in spacious tanks where visitors could use remote radio controls to maneuver replicas of warships, historical sailing vessels, and multi-oared Roman galleys. The types of models were legion: tugboats, ferries, British and U.S. destroyers, even Noah's Ark.

Left: Charles and Joy Stock pose aboard *Shoal Waters* at the International Festival of the Sea. Above: The cover of Charles' book, *Sailing Just for Fun: High Adventure on a Small Budget,* shoes *Shoal Waters* aground in the mud of the Thames Estuary; a pair of muddy mud boots are draped over the stern.

Without a doubt, the most impressive was the nearly 500 tiny boats built by one craftsman over, Philip Warren, starting in 1945. These miniatures are dubbed The Matchstick Fleet because they are made of balsa wood from wooden matchstick boxes at a scale of 300:1. The collection includes at least one vessel from each class of British warship, plus the recently launched *USS Winston S. Churchill.*

A view of some of Philip Warren's Matchstick Fleet at the International Festival of the Sea.

Epilogue

There's another part of this story that didn't happen. I had hoped to return to the U.S. on one of the SeaTrek tall ships. Whether or not I could gain passage was not determined until the day before their departure, and ultimately I didn't sail with them

While in England, I had pondered the emotions of Europeans who left their families and homeland to settle in America in the 1700 and 1800s. Back in Michigan, as our nation and the world experienced the events on and following September 11, 2001, I wondered what emotions the modern SeaTrek voyagers—many of them American citizens—may have felt as they entered New York Harbor on October 4 and sailed past New York City's terrorist-altered skyline.

On the SeaTrek website, I learned that the passengers aboard those tall ships had remained true to the intent and conditions of the historic voyage they were replicating; specifically, they had chosen to electronically disconnect from the news of the world. They did not know of the attack on the World Trade Center until they sailed into New York Harbor on October 4.

I also found answers to my question about their emotions in passengers' journals posted on the website. One wrote, "We sailed past ground zero. We saw the black smoke still billowing from the fires beneath the rubble of what used to be the majestic Twin Towers. Someone had a picture of the New York skyline, the way it used be. We held it up to the newly formed skyline. How could they have possibly disappeared? Up ahead was our symbol of hope and freedom— the Statue of Liberty. As I saw her there, her torch held high, an overwhelming sense of love and gratitude welled up in my heart and overflowed through my tears."

That tragedy of September 11, enacted with the aid of jumbo aircraft on buildings in the largest city in our land, reminded me, once again, of the significance of our maritime history, whether during times of peace or war. There is something simple about sailing the water; something fundamental about propelling a boat with wind, sticks, and rags; something solemn, joyous, and inspiring about the International Festival of the Sea, which in a primal way honored that watery element of our human heritage. Would I go to the festival again? Yes, in a heartbeat.

Porkies
(a *true* short story)

"You have porkies in the United States, don't you?" Gerald asked me, drawing out his vowels—"poooorkieees"—as much as he clipped his consonants. We were sitting in the Life Boat Inn—"A Family Beer Garden, Dogs Allowed"—near the beach on South Hayling Island. A black Lab curled under a pub stool next to the bar. "You know, white lies or April Fools? You have those in the States, don't you?" I nodded, wondering where Gerald was leading me.

My last full day in England, the day after the festival, had been leisurely. I had slept, read, and waded on the beach. As afternoon waned, I had explored clustered rows of colorful beach huts—about ten feet by ten feet in which people store beach chairs and other paraphernalia—and came upon a bright yellow and white cement block building with a sign that promoted "hot sugared donuts with the less-fattening center." I ordered two and tea; the former, served fresh from a deep fryer and the latter, in a hand-washed china cup.

While slowly enjoying this refreshment, I learned the proprietors, Gerald and Valerie Fuller, had been married nearly 50 years and had two children and six grandchildren. Gerald had been a grocery store manager and flew to the United States to visit supermarkets in the 1960s. Later, the couple owned and operated several stores, including the Creek Road Bakery. This beach kiosk was their—or was it his?—"retirement business."

Warming to conversation, Gerald was quick to share stories, which lasted through ales in two pubs and supper in the couple's home. Through it all, Gerald demonstrated a knack for blending truth with porkies and eyeing me keenly as I attempted to distinguish one from the other.

"You know those forts out on the Solent. You can see them from shore, you know. Those are Palmerston's Follies. He was prime minister back in the 1800s during the French Wars, and they're called Palmerston's Follies because they were never used. You can buy one, you know. For a million pound note. They unscrew them every 25 years to let the water out. Left-hand thread."

He continued, "When the *Queen Mary* used to come into Southampton, when it came over the horizon and we were on the beach at Hayling, all the visitors would stand up and wave. Grannies would shout, 'Look, Mary. There's the *Queen Mary*.' But the locals would pack up their stuff and get back to the top of the beach because they knew in *exactly* ten minutes there would be a six-foot wave come in from the wash of the *Queen Mary* and all the sandwiches and buckets and things would get washed away. It was great excitement." Gerald chuckled. "That's true. I know. I was on the beach."

He showed me a newspaper dated April 1, 1988. An article on the front page told of plans to build an entertainment establishment that would feature topless dancers and change Hayling's image of "Coasta Geriatrica." The article mentioned Gerald Fuller, of the Creek Road Bakery, as the person from whom shares of stock in the project could be purchased.

I asked Gerald how he got his name in the article. "I wrote it!" he replied. I looked at the byline—Joe Kerr. "Joker," he explained. "Now that's a porkie. An April Fool, you know."

He handed me another newspaper. An article displayed a large photo of Gerald standing in front of his bakery and photos of four men, all small mug shots. "This is not a porkie. This is truuuuee. I had a shop on Creek Road. A bakery. In 1987, they had a general election, and it was in June. Well, that was the beginning of the tourist season here. So, I said to the wife, 'We've got to advertise. There's no good in people just finding us; we've got to tell 'em we're here.' The election was announced, and I said, 'Why not stand for Parliament?' And I did."

"You mean you ran for office."

"Right. Right. We call it 'standing.'"

"Standing? For a seat?"

"Right. Right. Standing. Anyway, it cost 500 pounds for the deposit, which I knew I'd lose. But a piece in the local paper—four inches by one column—is about 40 quid. You don't get many of those for 500 pounds, do you? And how many people read them? Nought, nought, nought one percent. But, I thought, 'Well, for 500 quid, you get free delivery by the postman for a leaflet to every household. You get your name on notices. You get a bit of TV coverage.'

"So, I called myself the Creek Road Fresh Bread Party, because I had a bakery. This is not a porkie, you know. This is true. My platform was 'eat fresh bread daily.' I got 373 votes. That's 373 dedicated customers.

"Now, you can see our election on TV—of what happens when the thing's announced. The one who wins stands up and thanks the police and everyone else. Then the next one has a go, and slags off the one who won. The third one slags off him. And the next one, that sort of thing.

"Are you saying 'slags off?'"

"Slags off, you know. Has a go at them."

"You mean like taking a jab or a poke?"

"Yeah. That's right. Of course. We call it slagging over here."

"They don't just concede."

"Ohhhhh, nooooo!!! They *never* concede. They slag. This is England, you know. Anyway. The fellow who controls the election count is called the Returning Officer, and he came to me and said, 'Mr. Fuller, you don't want to speak, do you?' I said, 'Of course, I do! It's my last chance to aaadvertiiiiise!' I was the only one to get a cheer and a clap."

Above: Gerald and Valerie Fuller pose next to their concession building on the South Hayling Beach where I purchased two donuts and a cup of tea. Left: Gerald Fuller poses with a loaf of bred in front of the Creek Road Bakery; this was his campaign photo when "standing" for a seat in Parliament.

"Did you slag at the others?"

"Noooo!!! There's no point in that."

"What did you say?"

"Oh, I can't remember now, but probably something like, 'I thank all the people who are seeing me here and hope that you all come to my shop and buy bread. I could use the money.' You know, something like that. But it's advertising, you know. They came to my shop. They bought bread. They talked about me. That's what it's about!!!"

Days later, after returning home, I logged onto the Internet and searched for "British Parliamentary Elections." There, I found a website, that credits Independent G. W. Fuller with an asterisk by his name and an explanation: "Fuller owned a bread shop in the constituency. He was the candidate of the 'Creek Road Fresh Bread Party.'"

So, at least that part of his story is true. Now, as to Palmerston's Follies and unscrewing them to let the water out, left hand thread, well …

Historical Maritime Expressions

"Shake a leg" was called by a British boatswain if he saw a human form lying in a raised hammock during daytime hours, a privilege allowed only to women. If the leg was a feminine leg, no problem. If the leg was a dirty, hairy, masculine leg, the man would be punished.

"You scratch my back, and I'll scratch yours" was a code among sailors who were directed to whip each other. The phrase means "Lay it on lightly, and I'll do the same for you."

"Flogging a dead horse" refers to whipping a man past the point of death.

A "gig" is any job of short or uncertain duration; the word applies to rowing a Cornish Pilot Gig in hopes of gaining a short job as a ship's pilot.

Horror, Not Glory

The British take great pride in their historic flagships, and rightly so. *H.M.S. Victory* and *H.M.S. Warrior* are tremendous ships with significant meaning. As one citizen said, "*Victory* represents our victory over the French and Spanish. We must never forget that."

Yet, there is another side to victory, another face to glory. That is the dark side of war—any war.

In the context of these grand naval vessels, it is the horror of living and fighting aboard a ship for never-ending months on end. At the International Festival of the Sea, interpretive guides aboard *Victory* and *Warrior* detailed day-to-day conditions.

"Breakfast was cold porridge, like wallpaper paste. The midday meal was the only hot meal—stew of beef, pork, or fish. They had to boil it because the meat was sometimes kept for 18 months or more. The evening meal was ship's biscuits—very nice when they were first made, but after a couple of weeks, were full of maggots or weevils. They also had tea, which was full of red worms. The men preferred to eat the evening meal in the dark. They carried about 50 tons of fresh water, which after a few weeks, became rancid and slimy. The ship's company over the age of 14 would rely on beer, rum, brandy, or wine."

"The boys on these ships were only seven. A boy's job was to go down and get the gunpowder and magazines during battle. They used boys because they were small and fast [headroom on the lower stowage decks is less than five feet]. The boys were taught schoolwork. So, by the time they were 14, they could read and write and do navigation. A lot of the boys stayed on and became officers."

"They sometimes had women and children on these ships. These were unofficial passengers. At least two women are known to have given birth during the height of battle."

"For punishment of a lesser crime, a sailor would be shackled for 100 days in a position where he could still contribute to the operation of the boat from a seated position between the cannons. For punishment of a greater crime, a sailor would be shackled for one day and given enough leather and lashing to make a cat o' nine tails that would then be used to whip him. After 12 lashes, it would open a man's back. After 24, you could see bones. Once the punishment was finished, they cut him down and took him below to see the doctor who would pour salt into the wounds. This wasn't punishment; salt was the only antiseptic. The whip was used once on only one man, then thrown over the side."

from over there. You can see why everybody had ruptures in those days. In the stores on this ship, there were 350 trusses."

"The Royal Navy could fire one of these guns every 90 seconds. The French and Spanish, every five minutes. It wasn't that the French and Spanish were useless, but they were trained differently. If the English fired all 104 guns every 90 seconds, they would use 150 tons of gunpowder in nine-and-a-half hours."

"When you fired these guns, you put your ball and powder at a ratio of three to one—a 24 pound ball and an eight pound charge. The ball would leave the gun at 2,000 feet per second at a distance up to a mile-and-a-half. This would also give you a recoil of up to 60 feet if it was unimpeded by this

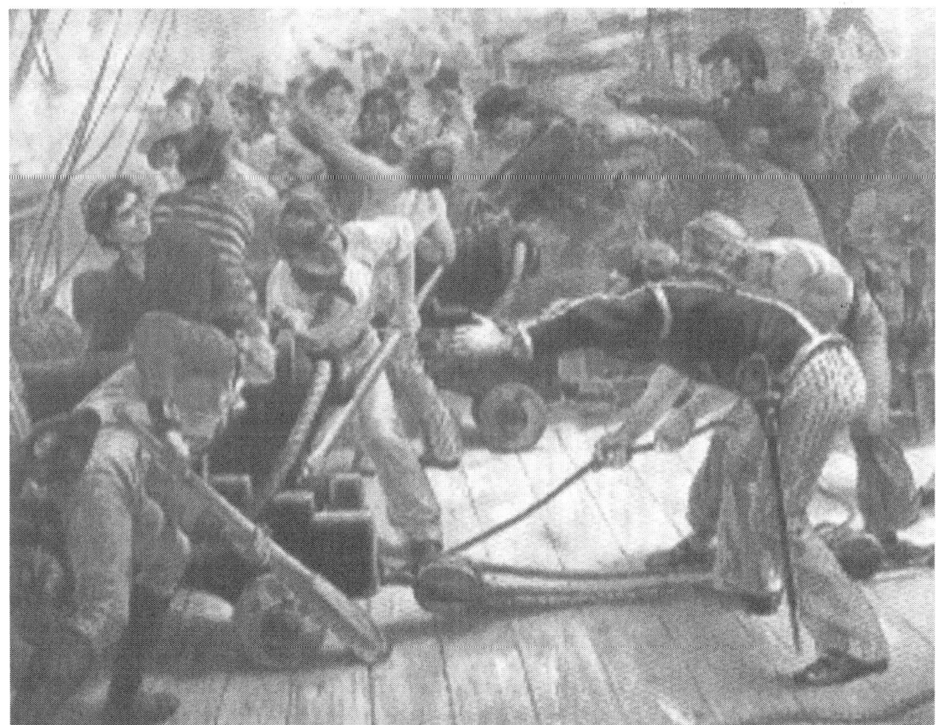

"The guns weigh five and a quarter tons. The barrel itself weighs two tons. They used to take the barrels off after they'd been fired about six times. It was so hot, you couldn't put any more gunpowder in. With manual block and tackle, they would just sling the barrel up and take it to the other side of the boat and bring a barrel

two-inch diameter breaching rope, which was measured so the front end of the gun would recoil just enough to put in a position to be cleaned and reloaded. The enemy's ships were very close. So, if you tried to clean and reload with the gun in firing position, snipers would hit you with shots from their muskets."

Old Gaffers
Solent Sound Race

During my first day at IFOS, I took a photograph of *Vagabond*, a 46-foot wooden trawler. When I introduced myself to owner David Cade, he invited me aboard for some tea. David proudly told me the history of his craft, a "classic pre-war motor cruiser" built in 1936.

He said the flotilla of nearby wooden sailboats were part of the Old Gaffers Association, of which he was president. As fortune would have it, the Old Gaffers were to hold their annual race on Solent Sound the next day. I invited myself along, and David introduced me to Joe Lester, skipper of *Iseult.*

Iseult, is a double-masted wooden ketch, 93 years old, 53 feet long with the bow sprit, that displaces 28 tons. More romantically, the legendary Iseult and her lover Tristram are characters of Celtic folklore. But, alas, this knight of King Arthur's Round Table died in battle, and his star-crossed lover, upon seeing him on his deathbed, assumed the same demise at her own hand.

Fortunately, for us, the race on Solent Sound was more favorable. We anchored in non-existent air near the starting line for nearly an hour, engaging in more tales of the sea while waiting for the wind to fill in. When it did, nearly 50 boats—from 14 to 54 feet, carrying traditional off-white or rust-red sails—set out for a 25-mile race on nearby parts of the Atlantic Ocean.

The day was glorious. The wind was propelling but not overpowering, and we hoisted a mainsail, topsail, jib, and spanker up stout wooden masts. The course was historic, taking us past three large stone forts two miles off the Portsmouth shore; these forts, Gerald Fuller would later tell me, were the structures he called "Palmerston's Follies." (See "Porkies" story.)

The international flavor was intriguing as ferries, the size of ocean liners, transversed our path and cast us in their lee en route to and from France.

Plus, I have never eaten so well aboard a vessel while racing: pickled onions, thick zesty potato chips, pork pies, tangy roasted chicken, and tea, of course, served by first mate Pat Lester from the boat's spacious galley.

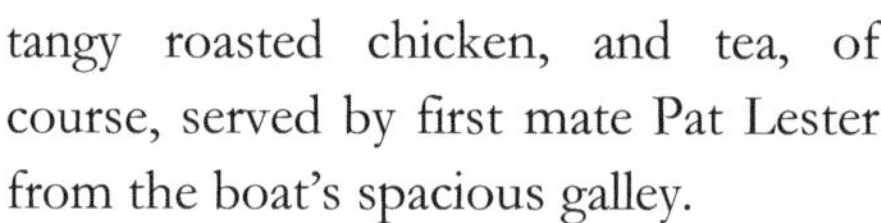

We finished somewhere in the middle of the fleet. Learning the winner was not a priority—just being on the water and sailing *Iseult* the best we could was all that mattered.

Coming back, the Old Gaffer fleet sailed through the bustling harbour amidst more international ferries, tiny pleasure craft, modern cruising yachts, chartered sailboats, tugboats and fishing boats, and rubber pontoon motor rafts aboard which coastal patrol officers shouted orders to small maneuverable craft to give way to larger vessels.

From the harbour and with the afternoon sun easing toward the horizon behind us, we were treated to an afterglow waterside view of tall ships, mostly back or white with glistening gold ornamentation, and the massive gray military vessels.

Top photo: The cabin on *Vagabond.* Center photo: The crew of *Iseult*; Joe Lester is second from right; Pat Lester is not shown. Bottom photo: a gaff-rigged sailboat, with all sails flying, is heeled over sharply in strong winds during the annual race on Solent Sound.

Pride of Baltimore II

A Bit of American Maritime Heritage

"The 1812 War put the United States on the world map," says Captain Jan Miles of *Pride of Baltimore II*, a traditional topsail schooner, built with raked masts after the fashion of Baltimore Clippers of the late 1700s and early 1800s. Captain Miles elaborates that these fast, sleek, sailing vessels helped raise the status of the, then, 35-year-young nation above the image of "a bunch of rag-tag rebel colonies." That was also the war during which Francis Scott Key wrote "The Star Spangled Banner" as the British attempted to bombard Fort McHenry..

The Baltimore Clippers, built in the Chesapeake Bay area, were capable of a very fast 15 knots. They couldn't carry as much cargo as slower sail-powered commercial vessels, but they captured a market niche by delivering time-sensitive, light-weight, profitable products.

At the start of the War of 1812, the "Second War of Independence," the tiny U.S. navy lacked sufficient warships to protect seagoing traders. President James Madison commissioned private merchant vessels into service with instructions to harass British commercial vessels off the U.S. coast, a practice that became a flourishing freelance business. Thus, these "privateers" were really government-sanctioned *pirates* who captured or sank 1,700 British vessels in the Atlantic and Caribbean.

One boat, *Chasseur*, was 116 feet stem to stern and blessed with a bold captain, Thomas Boyle, a brave crew of 115 men, and 16 cannons. *Chasseur* sailed to England and so disrupted British commercial ships in European waters that the Royal Navy assigned several warships to track her down. They were never able to do so, and *Chasseur* was affectionately dubbed "The Pride of Baltimore."

Interestingly, the Baltimore Clippers were not built from plans but by instinct, expertise, and Yankee ingenuity. None of the original Baltimore Clippers have survived the dry rot of peacetime inactivity. But *Pride of Baltimore*, the predecessor of *Pride of Baltimore II*, was built in 1977 with the same kind of ingenuity by skilled boat builders who, with an historical bent, pored over photos of those much-acclaimed vessels.

Pride of Baltimore served her purpose as a vessel of "friendship and goodwill" on behalf of the city of Baltimore until being lost at sea in the spring of 1986 north of Puerto Rico. Public mourning in Baltimore and Maryland led to construction of a replacement.

The keel for *Pride of Baltimore II* was laid in May, 1987, and the vessel was commissioned in October, 1989.

This successor ship is similar in design to her modern predecessor, but in the tradition of the original Baltimore Clippers, is also different: larger and heavier with more sail area, greater crew and passenger comforts, and state-of-the-art electronics.

Pride of Baltimore II continues to be a public relations vessel, plying the Great Lakes—where she spent the summer of 2001—and the Atlantic and Pacific to promote interest in the ships of the early American nation and the "friendship and goodwill" of the state of Maryland.

This photo of the author was taken aboard *Pride of Baltimore II* while docked in the harbor at Racine, Wisconsin. Robert Weir also sailed aboard *Pride* under Captain Jan Miles from Port Huron to Ogdensburg, New York, including through the locks at the Welland Canal.

Las Vegas to Oceanside, Naturally

First tip: Skip The Strip.
Too much glitter and glitz.
Too much consumptive waste.
Too much encroachment on delicate desert environment.
Instead, slip out to nature.

When my friend Cindy Gremban asked me to accompany her to the June wedding of her son Eric and his bride Maria in California, I said sure. The wedding was to be in Temecula, low-mountain wine country southwest of Los Angeles. Being adventuresome, Cindy and I decided to camp during the week prior—in canyons, deserts, mountain tops, and beaches. "Everything except a rain forest," Cindy said.

Come along. Ride with us. We'll take you to the out-of-doors wedding and introduce you to people and places we encountered along the way.

Kalamazoo, Chicago, Vegas

With both backcountry apparel and formal wedding attire packed, Cindy and I drove from Kalamazoo to Chicago on Saturday, June 6. We boarded a flight at Midway, followed the sun, and secured our rental car in Las Vegas two hours before sunset. Great. We would pick up a can of fuel for our camp stove and head out to the desert.

Not so easily done, however. The first mega store was sold out of the type of fuel we needed; the second mega store didn't carry it; and the third, a sporting goods outlet, had the right product but it only came packaged with a stove. Forty dollars lighter and with a second stove we wouldn't use, we noticed darkening dusk and our own grumbling tummies.

In-N-Out Burger

Solution: an In-N-Out Burger, one of Cindy's traditions when traveling to the Southwest. What's natural about fast food, you might ask. The answer: all-natural ingredients. Founded by Harry and Esther Snyder in 1948, the In-N-Out Burger has maintained its original simple fare: only burgers, fries, and drinks free of additives, fillers, and preservatives.

The beef comes from premium cattle, is packed and made into patties by in-house butchers, and shipped daily to 233 franchises in Utah, Arizona, Nevada, and California. The web site claims total freshness. "We don't even own a microwave, heat lamp, or freezer," it states.

The Strip

Our appetites were sated, but the sun had long passed over the mountains, leaving full darkness overhead. It was Saturday night. Okay, let's cruise the strip. Why not? Well, one hour and 2.5 miles of stop-and-go-and-stop-then-stop-some-more traffic later, we could offer plenty of reasons: pedestrian crowds, garish architecture and theme lighting, blaring noise, openly promoted prostitution. Nothing natural. Once we cleared the last traffic light, we were outta there.

Red Rock Canyon Campground

Thirty minutes later, we set up camp under a host of bright stars and a growing, nearly full moon. Warm, dry wind blew gently through the canyon. With low, low humidity, there was no need for a rain fly. And sleep came quickly and peacefully.

Paul Foster and Bobby Alvarez

While eating breakfast the next morning, I noticed two men organizing rock climbing gear at the neighboring campsite. Paul Foster had been climbing for 22 years, and Bobby Alvarez for 2.5; they had driven 250 miles from their homes in California to climb at Red Rock. The previous day, they spent 12 hours ascending Epinephrine, a 2,200-foot chimney that Paul called "a stimulating climb," thus its name, a synonym for adrenaline.

"All climbs have descriptive names," said Paul. "No Mistake. Big Pancake. Edging Skills or Hospital Bills." On the day we talked, they were going to "take it easy" with a few ascents of less than 100 feet each. "Climbing is as diverse as life," Paul philosophized.

Paul Foster and Bobby Alvarez hold some of the many carabiners they use for climbing at Red Rock Canyon.

Red Rock Canyon Scenic Loop

The Red Rock Canyon National Conservation Area encompasses 197,000 acres within the Mojave Desert. Located 20 miles west of Las Vegas, it features wild horses and burros, big horn sheep, cacti, petroglyphs, pictographs, and ample samples of rich red rock escarpment, hundreds of feet in height, that are often contrasted ivory white or pale gray striations.

The 13-mile scenic loop ascends 1,000 feet from the visitors center to the mid point, topping out at 4,721 feet above sea level. Numerous parking areas permit opportunities for photography, short walks, hiking, and rock climbing.

Molly Sheridan

At one of these scenic overlooks, we met Molly Sheridan, a tall, slender blonde who appeared to be in her 30s. "I started running late in life, at 48," she said, adding that she was now 52.

The 13-mile loop was part of Molly's daily training regimen as she prepared for the Bad Water Ultramarathon. With a distance of 135 miles in Death Valley in mid-July and an elevation gain of 13,000 feet, it is touted as "The World's Toughest Foot Race." Entrance is by invitation only. Molly, who has run for six days across the Sahara in the Marathon des Sables—carrying her own backpack and water, no less—was to be one of 86 competitors. Of the expected 120-degree heat, she says, "The human body is amazing; it acclimates."

Checking the Bad Water website in late July, I saw that Molly ran 131 miles in 45:09:17, stopping four miles short of the finish line because of a forest fire that forced evacuation of the area.

She earned an award for having completed the race in less than 48 hours. Her only rest was a ten-minute nap after 40 hours of running.

Mojave National Preserve

Thirty miles south, Cindy and I eschewed Interstate 15 and took the scenic two-lane road through the Mojave National Preserve, a 1.6 million-acre park of desert solitude. With topography of canyons, mountains, and mesas, its human-made features include abandoned mines, homesteads, and military outposts. A U.S. Department of Interior website describes its natural beauty as "singing sand dunes, volcanic cinder cones, Joshua tree forests, and carpets of wildflowers."

Joshua Tree National Park

On Sunday night, we camped at the Barker Dam Camp in the heart of Joshua Tree National Park, a 558,000-acre wilderness area that features gorgeous, scaleable boulders that nature has piled 50 to hundreds of feet high in artistic formation.

The park is named for its most notable vegetation, the sparsely branched Joshua tree, a giant member of the lily family whose botanical relatives include flowering grasses and or chids. It reminded me of Truffula trees in *The Lorax* by Dr. Seuss even though his book was inspired by the Monterey cypress.

In the morning, we walked and ran three miles to Barker Dam, a rain-fed basin accessible only through narrow canyon passageways. The natural rock formation was augmented with a concrete dam for cattle around 1900. Today, park wildlife drink from there—when water is present, that is. It was dry and looked like it had been dry a long time; we laughed at signs, embedded in dusty ground, that warned: "No Swimming."

Cholla Cactus Garden

Descending and letting the car coast at a comfortable 45 mph toward the southern edge of Joshua Tree, we encountered a majestic sight at the Cholla Cactus Garden where acres of sun-drenched silver-white cacti—and some mahogany brown from age—adorn the landscape.

Standing up to four feet tall, these immobile desert dwellers appear adorable with uplifted teddy bear arms and delicate yellow cup-like blossoms shaped like raspberries. But signs at the entrance to a narrow trail offer a strict warning: "Do No Touch."

Each spear is razor-sharp and barbed. Small sections of the stalk can break off and adhere to clothing and skin; removal is nearly impossible and painful.

Palm Springs Aerial Tramway

On Tuesday, we drove Interstate 10 into a 25-mph headwind through the San Gorgonio Pass, which features a wind farm with over 4,000 wind generators. Our destination was Mt. San Jacinto, by way of the Palm Springs Aerial Tramway.

The tram's valley station in Chino Canyon sits at an elevation of 3,500 feet from which cable cars ascend more than a mile, nearly vertically at a rate of 21 mph, to the mountain station at 10,801 feet. The change from the hot desert Sonoran life zone to the arctic/alpine life zone occurs in a mere 15 minutes—translation: we needed more than shorts and t-shirt at the top.

Mt. San Jacinto State Park

After a reasonably priced, sumptuous meal at Peaks Restaurant, which offers a terrific view of the valley, we set out with backpacks to Tamarack Valley Camp, 2.5 miles away with an elevation gain of 1,300 feet. Darkness arrived before we made that distance, so we chose the safe alternative and pitched our tent in the first reasonably level spot.

The next morning, we complimented our wisdom for not having attempted to go farther over roots and rocks the night before. Reality also told us we would not attain the summit of San Jacinto Peak before needing to return to the valley below. Yet, we pressed on amid lush ferns, wildflowers, and giant conifers in various stages of growth and decay.

Our reward was a spectacular above-the-clouds view of lower surrounding peaks at Wellmans Divide, followed by a sun-drenched traverse along an angular path of low shrubs salted with white boulders.

Robert Weir takes a break to enjoy the fresh air at Wellman's Divide, elevation 9,720 feet. Photo by Cindy Gremban

But our watches and the midday sun told us it was time to turn around. We had a dinner date with Eric and Maria that night, at sea level, in Oceanside.

The Melting Pot

The Melting Pot restaurant serves fondue like we had never seen. The first course was a pot of cheese, kept warm with burners set into the table, along with bread and fruit. The second course was a selection of raw meat, seafood, and vegetables that we skewered and lowered into boiling hot water for one to two minutes. Dessert was, you guessed it, melted chocolate into which we dipped bananas, strawberries, marshmallows, cake, and brownies. With 142 locations in 37 states, The Melting Pot is a unique fine-dining treat.

Camp Pendleton

The Del Mar Recreation Beach at Camp Pendleton provides 28 cottages and over 100 campsites for military personnel, reservists, and Department of Defense civilians. Cindy, who works for the Defense Logistics Agency in Battle Creek, is one of the latter; she reserved our campsite. We were not alone, but while all other "campers" came with luxury RVs, we were the only ones in tents.

Dropping into sleep with the sound of Pacific Ocean waves at night was serene. But waking to Marines exercising at daybreak was, well, interesting. Their sounds included callisthenic-induced grunts as well as rhythmic cadences as columns of men and women ran along the firm, tide-soaked sand. Physical training is part of a Marine's occupation, an activity they engage throughout the day. Eric described for us the Marine's "warrior athlete" semi-annual combat readiness exam, which he, at age 25, has completed in half of the allotted time.

- Event one: run 880 yards in boots and camouflage utilities in 3 minutes, 48 seconds (males) or 4 minutes, 34 seconds (females).
- Event two: lift a 30-pound ammunition can from below the chin to above the head 45 times (males) or 20 times (females) in two minutes.
- Event three: dash for 25 yards, drop to the ground and high crawl for 10 yards, then low crawl for 15 yards; get up and run zig-zag

through pylons for 25 yards; drag another Marine (a simulated casualty) for 10 yards, then pick up the Marine and carry for 65 yards; set the Marine down and pick up a 30-pound ammunition can and run for 50 yards, zig-zag for 25 yards through pylons; set the can down, pick up an inert grenade and lob it at a target 20 yards away, drop to the ground, and perform three pushups in 3 minutes, 29 seconds (males) or 4 minutes, 57 seconds (females).

Ocean Sailing

On Wednesday, Eric, Cindy, her friend Gee McNease, and I went aboard the 35-foot sloop *Gringo* for two delightful hours sailing off the coast of Oceanside. The winds were light as Captain Monte C. Yearley unhooked the dock lines. With mainsail already raised, we slipped out of the slip, through the harbor, and out to the Pacific.

A harem of at least two dozen sea lions barked from the platform of a navigational buoy, and we sailed toward them for a closer look before tacking out to sea.

Eric Gremban, Gee McNeese, Robert Weir, and Cindy Gremban sail aboard the sloop *Gringo*. Photo by Monte C. Yearly

Conversation was light and jovial, as it should be in the peaceful environs of gently rolling waves, as we took turns steering the boat.

Luis, Evelyn Centeno and Family

Luis and Evelyn are Maria's parents. Born and raised in the Philippines, Luis worked as a bank accountant and Evelyn as a registered nurse in a hospital operating room. They immigrated to the United States in 1991 when partial loss of vision caused Luis to no longer distinguish numbers on his ledger sheets. They also viewed the U.S. as "a great opportunity" for Maria and her younger brother, Alex.

Through friends, the family became pizzeria owners. Today, they own a diner that specializes in pizzas and American fare as well as Linbrook Bowl, a 40-lane bowling alley in which it is housed.

Luis and Evelyn don't bowl, but they enjoy watching bowlers, something they can do around the clock because their alley is one of three in California that is open 24/7. They have 40 employees, but make most of the pizzas themselves.

Their home in Anaheim, not far from Disney Land, is warm and friendly, made of brick and slate roof, with an outdoor pool, patio, and garden that features flowers, vegetables, an orange tree, and a persimmon tree.

That night, with a carryout pizza in the backseat, we drove to the San Diego Airport and picked up Cindy's younger son, Derek, then took him and the pizza to Eric and Maria.

Ocean Kayaking

The next day, Thursday, Cindy and I rented kayaks from La Jolla Kayak. Our guide, Ashley, led us and six others on a tour of the Seven Caves off the coast of La Jolla. The rollers were gentle so we entered one of the caves, a thrilling experience facilitated by Ashley who swam with fins behind each kayak as she steered us in and out one at a time.

Eric and Maria's Wedding

Friday morning, we broke camp and drove an hour inland to Temecula in the heart of Southern California's wine country. Rehearsal that afternoon and the outdoor wedding on Saturday took place at the vineyard of Wiens Family Cellars.

Eric and Maria's choice was excellent. They were married in the company of family and friends, many of them Marines, in the glow of late afternoon sun with a backdrop of grapevines and mountains.

The ceremony was sincere, the service supreme, the food fantastic, and the wine divine.

Best of all, the love energy was genuine, permeating all. Luis and Maria shared a special dance, as did Cindy and Eric who, in a supreme gesture of tribute typical of a Marine, dropped to one knee in front of his mother and bowed as the song ended.

Then we all danced. Even those who were prone to sit on the sidelines received encouragement from others and joined in.

At ten, the DJ played the last song, Billy Joel's "Piano Man," and everyone came to the floor. We formed a circle, arms across shoulders, sang and swayed. Eric and Maria stepped into the center and danced, and we honored them. Then, they reached out to their parents and family who joined them. They invited bridesmaids, groomsmen, and close friends, and the dancing couples numbered a dozen while the rest of us joined hands to retain the surrounding circle.

And this was the most beautiful moment of the entire trip—the moment when love flows naturally, as it was meant to do, among all of creation.

A Run with the Marines

By Cindy Gremban

You never know when a wonderful opportunity will present itself. I have run the Chicago Marathon, a local triathlon, and the Kal-Haven Trail from Kalamazoo to Lake Michigan. But nothing will ever compare with my experience running with the Marines!

My son Eric, who is a Marine, was getting married on June 13 2009. My friend Bob and I were camping at Camp Pendleton prior to the wedding. Every morning, I went for a run along the ocean and saw groups of Marines running, exercising, and playing sports to build strength, endurance, and discipline. They were in great shape.

On Friday, I met a very large group of Marines and I decided to run with them. I assumed they would quickly run by me. However, I was inspired and picked up my pace while listening to this male choir of more than 200 voices as they "sang" their various cadences.

When Marines run in a group, one person shouts a statement, such as, "One, Two, Three, Four," and the group answers in a rhythmic manner, "Marine Corps." The leader may then shout, "Next came the color gold," and the group responds, "Marine Corps." Sometimes the leader will shout "feels good" or "sounds good" or "fired up" or "here we go." The group then repeats the cadence. It was difficult for me to understand some of the words, but my main memory was the powerful energy and the full sound of the strong Marine voices.

Cindy Gremban (far left with cars in the background) runs with a column of more than 200 Marines at Camp Pendleton, California.

. On this morning, there was such a long line of Marines that three different cadences sounded at the same time. There was this incredible male choir and the sound of the magnificent Pacific Ocean. I could have run forever with these brave, inspirational men.

I began running at a distance to stay out of their way, but I had questions. I ran up to the road guards, the two who run in front wearing reflective vests to stop traffic at intersections. These guys were so friendly—and welcomed my questions. I asked how many Marines were in this group and was told more than 200, an unusually large number to run together at one time.

Then I ran back to the guide in the front row, the one who carries the unit flag. As we ran, I chatted with the guide and the four others in the front row. They were respectful and encouraging.

As we neared our campsite, I asked the guide if I could get a picture. He was agreeable and told me where the group would be running after leaving the beach.

I quickly ran to our camp and asked Bob to bring his camera—and he took a picture of me running with the Marines through a parking lot.

Altogether, I ran about three miles with this wonderful group of motivational men. To them, it was just another run along the beach. To me, it was a once in a lifetime opportunity, and being with them instilled confidence.

In addition to being a Marine mom, I work for the Defense Logistics Agency, which supports the Marines and all the military. I am honored to have had this opportunity to run with these Marines who serve our country and represent values of honor, courage, and genuine respect.

Semper Fi.

A Traveler's Journey

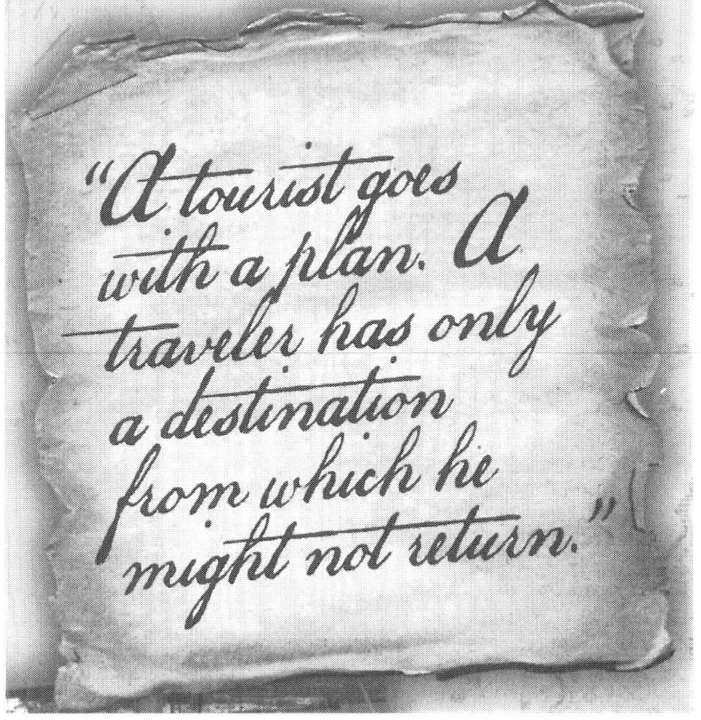

This story is of a journey to connect with interesting people of other nations. I visited Barbados, Spain, Greece, Bulgaria, Germany, Russia, and India. I sailed across the Atlantic and the Aegean, Black, and Baltic seas. I went as a traveler with much of my journey unplanned. I traveled alone and met many people—"travel angels"—who guided me along my way.

Chapter One: Barbados and the Atlantic … April 8 to 26, 2010

Wayne was a CouchSurfing host, a dark-complected man in his 60s who originated in Trinidad before moving to Canada in his 20s. He was to come to Barbados with his German girlfriend three decades ago, but when the Berlin Wall fell in 1989, she chose to reside in united Germany rather than with him in paradise.

He taught filmmaking at the University of the West Indies and produced movies but not of the Hollywood variety. "In Barbados, we make do with what we have; if we don't have it, we make it," Wayne said. He was working on a thriller, shot primarily in his two-room studio. I slept on the set amidst the sound of music from nearby bistros and chirping palm tree frogs.

Part of the set in Wayne's studio in which I slept.

Wayne took me to see three films. The first two were shorts by a Caribbean scriptwriter and producer about the influence of Indians and Africans on the islands of Trinidad and Haiti. The third was *Dead Man,* an early Johnny Depp flick, the storyline of which paled in comparison to the idyllic outdoor viewing venue: a 20-foot screen on the island's south beach, a soft breeze, lapping waves, and a dinner of tropical fish and good wine.

Having lost interest in the movie's morbid storyline, I conversed with **Lisbeth** (pronounced Lisbet), who registered guests at the cozy, two-story hotel—she called it an "apartment"—where the movie was shown. She was in her early 40s, had come from Venezuela 19 years earlier, and was still challenged by the island's numerous native and transplanted dialects. Her English was charming, with a pleasant rhythm, as we discussed physical health, spirituality, and human connectivity.

On my last morning in Barbados, I bought a coral necklace from **David**. I hadn't intended to do so, having already turned down requests by roaming beach vendors who hawked snorkeling, water skiing, and powerboat rides. But David was different. He and I met as we both, from opposite directions and with lunch in hand, approached the same makeshift bench that was nailed to a palm tree. There, gazing upon the azure sea, we sat and talked. He said I looked like a professor and asked if I worked for a local environmental organization that studied the sea and coral.

Then he showed me his necklaces, which he carried in a pouch. "My four children made them," he said. One

caught my attention. Now, I'm not big on souvenirs, and I was intent on traveling light, but this one, I rationalized, weighed practically nothing, could be worn, and would not require dusting. I chose not to haggle over the price of $20 Barbadian ($10 U.S.), in part, because David had already allowed me to take a close-up photo of his implanted tooth—gold with inset diamond—which he had found on the beach near a shipwreck.

Susie was the stewardess aboard the bus that took me from Wayne's studio to Barbados' deepwater port and the tall ship, *Royal Clipper,* that would carry me across the Atlantic. She collected my fare and placed the coins in a well-worn brown leather pouch that hung by a long strap around her neck, then, she helped me remove my 20-pound rucksack and 40-pound backpack and set them on the floor.

She was in her 40s, attractive with dark, native skin and bright eyes. Yet, her lips seldom smiled. And she spoke the Queen's English. In London, she worked as a nurse. She had returned to Barbados, to her place of birth, a year earlier to care for her dying mother.

With estate work nearly finished, Susie would soon depart, but her tone conveyed a desire to linger. "When you are a sensitive person, it is good to take time away; otherwise you get burned

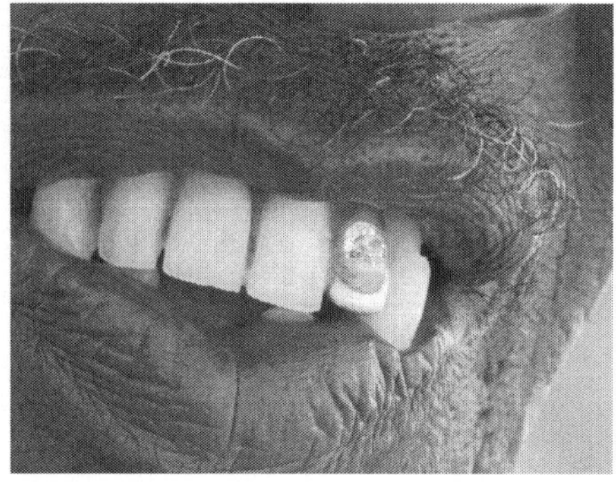

out," she said, conveying that she is a person who will continue to care for people no matter where she lives or works, whether bedside or on a bus.

Mariano was among *Royal Clipper*'s greeting crew. As a marine biologist, he would host daily lectures on aquatic life and serve on the ship's entertainment team. At that moment, he helped me connect to the seaport terminal Internet so I could send last-minute emails to a cadre of friends and clients for whom I was editing books.

We embarked that evening and, for the next 16 days, I connected with nature in the most expansive sense—far out of sight of land but afloat in a glorious vista of gently rolling ocean, sunshine, moonlight, clouds, wind that filled this magnificent vessel's five-masted rig and 42 sails, and dolphins that cavorted in our bow wake.

I also engaged in international conversation of the most stimulating nature with people from many European nations, South Africa, Great Britain, Canada, and the United States.

Royal Clipper, a luxury ship with sails, will carry 200 passengers, which she often does while cruising the Caribbean in winter and the Mediterranean in summer. But for this ocean voyage, we numbered 82 and were outnumbered by crew and service staff at a rate of two to one.

Traveling alone, I enjoyed exquisite cuisine with every English-speaking person (most of them were multi-lingual) and others with whom I could only communicate with smiles and gestures. Topics covered the waterfront of politics, education, healthcare, history, language, customs, and culture.

People from other nations were genuinely curious about the U.S. and knew a great deal about American history.

Bernhard from Germany had been a young man at the end of World War II when his city, Berlin, came under control of the Allies; with his home in the American sector, he learned and could recall much about the U.S. and its presidents.

Paul from the Netherlands, at 24, was the youngest adult passenger; with a touch of skepticism, he asked if people in the United States care what people from other countries think. I replied with my belief that Americans who engage common folk from other lands do, but many others, those entrenched in nationalism, do not.

Robin from the UK expressed his hope that Barack Obama be elected for a second term, and most agreed.

Jim from Canada stated his opinion that the U.S. "is a complicated country," which he observes with neighborly watchfulness. "Canada catches whatever the U.S. has got," he said.

Bob came from Media, Pennsylvania, a Quaker community I know well from having lived there while researching and writing my second book, *Peace, Justice, Care of Earth,* in 2005. However, it quickly became apparent that he and I travel in different philosophical circles. Yet, for each point on which we disagreed, we found mutual respect in our shared belief that all people are a part of the one, human race.

Trevor and **Margaret** and **Stephen** and **Ann** hailed from South Africa. The latter couple owned two dairy farms and milked 1,900 head of cattle; they were concerned about a political candidate who was telling citizens to kill farmers. The former couple had retired from a security business now owned by their son; they

spoke of car thieves who use AK-47s to shoot down security helicopters. These four wanted their country to return to the ways of apartheid.

Not every conversation was deep.

Aase from Germany taught me the fine art of signaling waiters and holding tableware and a wine glass, European style.

Joan, who at 93 was the oldest passenger, was among the few who climbed the ratlines to enjoy an elevated view from the crow's nest.

Doris from Germany spoke of having been married for 30 years to a man who thought a vacation was a visit to his family in Italy; since his death, she has been aboard numerous vessels, traveling more than being at home. "I started with the far-away places: Australia and New Zealand," she said.

Henning and **Gini** from Germany were aquatic consultants and marine architects who build inflatable sport boats and design diving gear. They have worked throughout the world and spoke knowledgeably of Lake Michigan and other parts of the U.S. In regard to my journey, Henning, who wears a black patch over his right eye—"Karma in this lifetime," he said of the injury—advised: "Be a benefit to everyone not just yourself. Compare but don't criticize. Absorb but don't copy. Enjoy new places but remember your roots."

When I thanked them for speaking English, he said that English is America's gift to the world because it's easy to learn and understand. "But that's only American English," he added, "not formal British English and certainly not Texas English."

Top: *Royal Clipper* under full sail. Middle: Murals on part of the companionway. Bottom: On the night of the captain's dinner, I dined with passengers from the United Kingdom, Canada, and Germany.

Chapter Two: Spain … April 26 to May 9, 2010

If set properly, a single sail can pull a ship o'er the seas, but untended sails will set a vessel adrift. In Spain, Internet and credit card disconnects could have made me feel like a castaway, but two shoreside people came to my rescue. One was Karim in Malaga, and the other was Josep, a long-time friend, in Barcelona.

While sailing tall ship *Royal Clipper* across the Atlantic, I was electronically out of touch for 16 days, so upon disembarking in Malaga, I wanted to contact friends and author clients for whom I was editing book manuscripts.

But, first, I needed lodging. Not having a reservation, I asked people on the streets for recommendations: some suggested the newer part of the city with its avenues and casinos, while others directed me to quaint Old Malaga.

I chose the latter and happened upon Carlos V, a hotel named after a ruler of the Holy Roman Empire and the Spanish Empire in the 1500s. Nested in the middle of a block, the establishment is a five-story structure with clean, comfortable, cozy rooms at very reasonable rates.

Not able to get online with my laptop there, I went in search of a *biblioteca* (library). Instead, at a *locaturio* (Internet café), Karim, a 24-year-old computer student from Morocco, found and fixed the problem in my Internet settings.

For the next five days, I mixed business with pleasure, working at Carlos V and taking long walks in this warm, charming Mediterranean community. Whether strolling alone or with Karim, who had offered to relate Arabian influence on Andalusian history, I found the narrow streets and wide plazas to be alive with people of all ages, day and night.

Located on the Mediterranean, Malaga is Spain's sixth most-populous city. It was founded by Phoenicians 2,700 years ago and has seen domain by Carthaginians, Romans, Arabs, and Spaniards.

Romano Teatro, a Roman theater built in the first through third centuries, was buried for nearly two millennia then rediscovered in 1951. With excavation still underway, public access was not allowed.

Looking through a chain link fence, we saw about 60 people, perhaps students, seated in the upper rows of the semicircular balcony. They appeared minuscule in comparison to the theater's stage and orchestra in the foreground and the adjacent edifices of Gibralfaro and Alcazaba that towered behind.

Alcazaba was built by the Arabs from the eighth to eleventh centuries; its name means a walled fortification within a city, which aptly describes this structure of brick and stone on the lower part of Malaga's tallest hill.

Gibralfaro, a castle erected by the Phoenicians in the fourteenth century, occupies the upper part of the same hill.

Our trek up, via stone incline, took us more than two hours. As Karim and I climbed, we experienced ever-changing vistas of Renaissance-designed government buildings, a tree-lined boulevard, a flower-patterned traffic circle, and the beaches of New Malaga in the distance.

Near the top, we gazed upon the harbor to the south, the Roman Catholic Catedral de Malaga and surrounding buildings to the west, and a bullring amid the city's modern hotels to the east.

At the apex, we visited a museum, roamed through gardens that included cacti and orange trees, and explored parapets that featured brick-patterned walkways and turrets with arrow loops through which we could see a valley, homes, and hills inland to the north.

We descended on a serpentine path toward a long, linear park populated with kiosks. The vendors there served food, beverages, and wares from distant lands: Egypt, Argentina, Peru, Brazil, Cuba, Galicia, Alamannia, and others.

A colorful sign extended a "welcome" in seven languages, displayed the flags of many nations, and marked this park as "Festival Intercultural." Karim explained that Malaga is a candidate in the European Capital of Culture competition.

Karim and I purchased dinner, sat on a bench under palm trees, and discussed history, religion, and philosophy as small night creatures chorused about us. Resurrecting Spanish words I had learned long ago in college, we began to speak in two languages. We parted close to midnight, but I wasn't tired and roamed the streets some more.

At Marques de Larios, a pedestrian mall, people strolled on a long red carpet rolled out for a film festival that had ended the day before, a Sunday. Their path was lit by ornate street lamps and lined with life-size placards of classic films.

Closer to my hotel, several eating establishments were open and serving patrons both inside and outside in this balmy clime, and street washers with a high-pressure water hose attached to a municipal truck went about their daily nocturnal chore.

Malaga's streets are made of contrasting shades of marble, stone, and tile in artistic patterns of squares, diamonds, circles, and chevrons. How might they have influenced Pablo Picasso who was born in Malaga in 1881 and lived there until he was 19?

On subsequent days, I toured Museo Picasso and Catedral de Malaga. The museum features drawings of nudes, minotaurs, and bacchanalia. The magnificent stone cathedral, built in the Renaissance style between 1528 and 1782, stands nearly 300 feet tall and contains 15 chapels and 24 altars.

On my fifth and final day in Malaga, Karim took me to his mosque. It was a holy day, and the inner chamber was nearly full and reserved for Muslims. Because this zealous youth had already attempted to convert me to his faith, he was disappointed that I could not worship next to him. Nevertheless, he removed his shoes and went inside while a greeter who spoke impeccable English directed me to a courtyard within the mosque, adjacent to the inner chamber.

This area had a marble floor lined by intricately carved Arabian arches and pale sandstone walls adorned with messages from the Koran. With deference to the custom of Islam, I removed my shoes.

More men arrived, dressed in long *jellabiya,* business suits, and athletic shirts that sported the names of American teams. Kneeling and prostrating on mats, they numbered two or three hundred and prayed loudly while I, not understanding the words, sat in a corner alcove, closed my eyes, and absorbed the rhythm of their chant.

Karim and I strike a similar pose outside the mosque where he worships.

One prearranged part of my trip was to attend the wedding of my friends Josep and Chus in Barcelona.

From Old Malaga, I took a bus to the train station where I boarded a high-speed train, part of the Spanish National Railway Network (RENFE), that left on time, traveled at 200 km/h, arrived on time, and provided complimentary ear plugs, eye shades, and bottled water for overnight travel. The next morning, Josep met me at the station and escorted me to his home.

In Barcelona, I discovered that my credit card companies had blocked my cards even though I had previously notified them I would be traveling in Europe. Using Josep's landline, I called the States and had the cards reactivated, which enabled me to make reservations for later, unplanned parts of my trip.

"Now you know the difference between a tourist and a traveler," Josep said. "A tourist goes with a plan; a traveler has only a destination from which he might not return."

Josep, an entrepreneur whose company provides turnkey computer systems for large businesses, and Chus, a teacher, live on the fifth, and top, floor of a modern condo in a high-density part of the city. They are happy people who intone the greeting, *ola,* like opening notes in a melody.

Walking with them to market, we passed a store-front church with youth chatting outside and numerous pedestrians patronizing small, close-quartered establishments: an auto repair shop with a single garage door, *locaturios,* clothing and shoe stores, flower retailers, and eateries.

"It's a working man's neighborhood," Josep stated, pointing out a corner bar where, on two evenings, we joined local patrons to cheer Barcelona in national soccer championship games.

While Josep and Chus prepared for their wedding, I walked the site of the 1992 Summer Olympics, a multi-hectare campus with numerous fields and facilities where youth practiced soccer and adults played cricket.

The promenade outside the Olympic stadium contains wide terraces, curving stone stairways, and water fountains drenched in golden lamplight. There, at sunset, the wind seemed to whisper of physical prowess imbued by the world's finest athletes of nearly two decades ago.

On other days, I visited Antoni Gaudi's unfinished cathedral; walked through Poble Espanyol, an outdoor architectural museum of full-size buildings from every region in Spain; and traveled by commuter train to Montserrat, a mountain monastery outside Barcelona.

Chus and Josep on their wedding day.

Throughout the city, people demonstrated their love of parks and efficient use of space. A car dealership on a main thoroughfare, for example, had minimized its geological footprint by showcasing its vehicles on the first two floors of a seven-story building while the upper levels were apartment homes with balconies adorned by bicycles, plants, laundry, and sun shades.

Josep and Chus' wedding took place at city hall in a matrimonial chapel that was as ornate as any church.

At the reception, Josep's father, two of Chus' uncles, and I engaged in a challenging conversation in Catalan, Spanish, French, and English. None of us knew more than one language well, so when one spoke, others translated what few words they could. As we gained understanding, our laughter and claps on the back became idioms in the universal language of fellowship and celebration.

Chapter Three: Historical Seas Tall Ships Regatta … May 9 to June 2, 2010

A woman near the airline boarding gate in Dusseldorf, Germany, pointed to two men and said, "Talk to them." She gestured toward the bag I was carrying emblazoned with an image of tall ship *Royal Clipper,* the vessel I had sailed across the Atlantic three weeks earlier. "They're sailors too."

The men were Klaus and Tom, volunteer crew for the German tall ship *Alexander von Humboldt.* During our layover in Nuremberg, we met 11 more sailors for that vessel. They, like I, were destined for Volos, Greece, and the start of the Historical Seas Tall Ships Regatta.

The Volos airport was primitive. The terminal, a single Quonset hut too small to hold all passengers from a single flight, had a baggage claim conveyor so short that only a dozen people could stand next to it. With the lengthy line of passengers waiting to enter on the runway side, another bulbous gathering of those who had collected their luggage and passed through the single exit to the parking lot, and the narrow strand of people squeezed inside, we simulated grains of sand in a horizontal hourglass.

Once through, we boarded a bus for the 40-minute ride into Volos, stopping once to avoid crossing the landing path of three F-16 fighter jets that were practicing touch-and-gos.

Volos, itself, is a beautiful seaside resort nestled between the Aegean Sea and inland mountains, idyllic for both sailing and skiing.

I stowed my gear aboard *Kaliakra,* the three-masted barquentine I would sail in the regatta. My berth was in a seven-foot by seven-foot cabin with that of Tony, the cook, who did not speak English.

Topsides, I heard drums, bagpipes, and glockenspiels. Playing "Jingle Bells"? In May? The musicians were sailors from two larger vessels in the regatta: *Shabab Oman* from Oman and *Dewaruci* from Indonesia.

A young man handed a blue t-shirt with the regatta emblem to me and said it was parade time. We hustled to the staging area then joined officers and crew from 21 ships, representing 15 nations. For the next hour, we walked and performed team-building antics in front of thousands of viewers along Volos' main shoreline artery.

The young man who had given the shirt to me was Stanislav Koludov, *Kaliakra*'s captain. He was 32, and this was his first captaincy. His previous assignment had been as the ship's first mate, responsible for all on-deck crew activities—and he still loved to lead from the deck, pulling lines and tweaking sails with the crew.

Most of the sailors were cadets, ages 18 to 22, who had signed a contract with Bulgarian maritime companies to

work for six years in exchange for four years of college education, a good barter. Many of the cadets had never been to sea before, yet they would soon climb aloft to furl sails many meters above the deck.

Captain Koludov was an excellent teacher. "The first rule is to never push," he said. "We are a racing ship. We do our best but we don't endanger people. When they have basic skills, we step them up to do more complicated things, and it becomes quite exciting."

Kaliakra, at a length of 171 feet and a beam of 26 feet, was built to be a sail training vessel, as were most ships in the regatta. "It's acknowledged worldwide that it's better for future officers to get their first voyages on a sailing ship where they are entirely dependent on the elements: wind and water," Captain Koludov explained. "The cadets learn to rely on each other and to follow orders. These are the basic skills needed to be a sailor for every ship."

Our embarkation from Volos was rife with pageantry as the fleet motored out of the harbor, raised sails, and passed thousands of people waving and cheering ashore. We were accompanied by dozens of pleasure craft, fishing vessels, and more than 50 rowers, modern Argonauts, aboard a replica of Jason's mythological *Argos.*

Kaliakra was the first vessel to cross the start line for the Volos-to-Istanbul leg of the regatta, an excellent start. With the sails and trimmed, the crew celebrated on the mizzen deck with a group photo. The view astern was of our competitors, also under full sail, falling away in the distance.

We raced for two days and nights until reaching the Dardanelles, the 50-mile strait that runs through European Turkey and Asian Turkey and connects the Aegean and Black seas. For another two days, we anchored with dozens of oth-

Left: *Kaliakra* sits at her dock in Varna, Bulgaria. Above: *Kaliakra*'s crew assemble on the vessel's aft deck for a photo to celebrate a successful start of the first leg of the Historical Seas Tall Ships Regatta. Next column: From our stern, we could see the magnificent tall ships sailing behind us.

er vessels of various sizes and purposes close to Istanbul. Then, we convoyed through the Bosporus, accompanied by several government security vessels and a helicopter.

The next day, we set sail again for the Istanbul-to-Varna leg of the race, being the second ship across the starting line and arriving at our destination three days later.

The atmosphere aboard *Kaliakra* was a pleasant blend of camaraderie and reverie. All of us, the Bulgarian crew and guest passengers from Greece and the U.S., stood watch twice a day: mine was noon to 4:00 pm and midnight to 4:00 am. The cadets spoke only Bulgarian, but with eye contact, hand signals, and a few key words, I learned to pull lines in sync with them.

Only four of the Greeks spoke English well. When I attempted to tell a joke, the punch line got lost in the translation, and nobody laughed.

Nikos, a Greek in his 40s who was vitally interested in politics, commerce, and international relations, spoke of his country's military regime of the 1960s and '70s and the populace's radical shift from being oppressed then to, now, having "excessive individual freedoms that endanger freedom for everyone."

He said that politicians skim "black millions" from public coffers to increase their personal wealth. Of the European Union's 110-billion-euro bailout of Greece a week before our departure, he said government officials were "idiots," then explained that that word comes from *idiotiki zoi*, which means "politicians who look after their own business rather than the public good."

Early one morning, about 2:00 am, Kostas and Kostas, two Greeks in their 60s whose cheeks and chins had become grizzled with the start of a beard, sang love ballads on the aft deck. The night was moonless, the sea dark, the wind light, and their basso voices dulcet.

On a sunny afternoon, Martin (pronounced Mar-teen), a Bulgarian cadet from Sofia, 800 kilometers inland from the Black Sea, who had never been on a boat before, brought a book to me. The book consisted of diagrams of our vessel's various masts, sails, arms, lines, stays, and shrouds. Each was identified by both its Bulgarian name and its English name. Martin spoke minimal English, but for the next three hours, he and I explored the vessel, learning key sailing words in each others' language.

On one page, Martin noted the martingale. "Wot ees theeese?" We went forward and peered over the bow at the vertical wooden pole that extended from the middle of the bowsprit to a cable running from the fore end of the bowsprit to the prow. I explained that its purpose was to hold tension on the cable. Martin said, "Eet ees my name." I told him the cable is called a bobstay and that "Bob" is the short form of my name. "Ooh, I really like that," he replied with a broad smile.

Moments like that made it hard to say good-bye to these young sailors after being at sea with them for 14 days, but the next part of my journey was at hand.

I stayed in Varna for ten days, luxuriating in a resort at ridiculously low off-season rates, watching a huge student parade to honor saints Cyril and Methodius who created the Cyrillic alphabet, touring museums and waterfront parks, visiting a third-century cliff monastery, and fending off taxi drivers who insisted I needed a ride even if I were walking a short distance.

I also learned, much to my surprise, that, because I was an American *in situ*, I could not buy a Euro rail pass. So I spent several days attempting to book an airline reservation out of the country. That process was hampered by Bulgaria Air's computer system that refused American credit cards, inconvenient telephone communications, and booking agents (when I finally reached them) who told me to simply bring enough cash and buy my ticket at the airport gate.

Upon learning I could not fly out of Varna, I bused to Sophia and enjoyed a one-day, whirlwind tour of government buildings, museums, churches, and historical monuments with a Bulgarian friend I had met in the U.S. five years earlier.

Fortunately, only two days before my flight, an airline supervisor said the computer system was fixed, so I bought a ticket for a reasonable fare. With a sigh of relief, I flew to Germany, a country I had not planned to visit.

The famous Russian training vessel *Mir* passes *Kaliakra* as the sun sets on the Black Sea.

Chapter Four: A Spontaneous Stop in Germany, then to Russia via the Baltic Sea … June 2 to 19, 2010

Germany is rich with historical landmarks, especially in Berlin. The Wall, Reichstag, and Checkpoint Charlie draw visitors. But people become the focal point—some of them intentionally. At the Brandenburg Gate, for example, people make theatrical appearances costumed as uniformed American and Russian soldiers, Berlin Bear stands with a Doughboy and a WAC, a Jedi knight roams about.

These are human props, people with whom tourists pose and pay a euro or two for the privilege. A buckskin-clad Indian chief, sporting a full headdress and feathered pike, was born in Canada. He works this job six months each year. "But not when it's hot or cold. I had heart surgery," he explains. He collects 40 or 50 euros in tips per day.

The Memorial to the Murdered Jews of Europe, built in 2003–04, is a work of genius by Peter Eisenman. It consists of 2,711 coffin-size gray concrete slabs, called *stelae.* Around the perimeter, these are short, and people sit on them, eat, chat, and relax.

But walk into this massive memorial, 4.71 acres in size, and you feel the ground slope downward as the *stelae,* shoulder-width apart and arranged in strict ranks and files, become taller. Before you know it, you are literally and metaphorically in over your head. People cross your path then disappear. You hear voices. In the inhuman reality that this interactive memorial symbolizes, a fear-ridden nation might wonder: Are they talking about me? Might they turn me in? Might I also be taken and unwillingly "disappear"?

Even the floor consists of gray tiles and gray crushed stone, depicting shower tiles and grout. Were not showers, supposedly for cleansing, used for gassing persons considered "undesirable"?

Inside the Information Centre associated with this memorial, a map of Europe identifies 500 concentration camps, mass killing sites, and deportation points in almost all nations shown. The victims were not just Jews, nor were Germans the only perpetrators. How could so many murder so many? Displays at Topographie des Terrors Museum, another Berlin historical site, reveal that national demoralization after the Treaty of Versailles in 1919 caused economic and social collapse, and Germany became fertile ground for radical counterpoint. The Nazi Party merely sated popular demand.

Traveling by train from Berlin to Hamburg, my ticket assigns me next to a young German, Karsten Gold, an environmental engineer for a major airplane manufacturer. He was a soldier in the East German army when the Berlin Wall fell in November 1989. "We never thought that would happen," he says. Six months later, Germany reunified, and his tour of duty ended early. Karsten invites me to his home in the village of Himmelpforten; the name means Heaven's Gate and is a place to which people post letters to Santa Claus.

I fulfill the invitation a week later, traveling by commuter train from Hamburg an hour into German countryside. Karsten's wife, Hiltrud, prepares a delightful, simple meal, and the couple asks that I read a bedtime story to their three boys.

I give them postcards that depict Michigan, equating the state's shape with that of their hands. Karsten produces a globe and transforms the bedtime story into a geography lesson with emphasis on the relative locations of Germany and Michigan. Hiltrud gives me a jar of homemade *holunderblütengelle,* jelly made from elderberry flowers that she picked.

In Poppenbüttel, a Hamburg suburb, I am the guest of Gisela van Riesenbeck who I met two months earlier aboard tall ship *Royal Clipper*. She took an interest in my four-month, seven-nation journey and offered lodging for a week when I had no definite reservations.

In contrast, my earlier notion had been to take Eurail trains out of Bulgaria through major European capitals—touristing in daylight and traveling by night—to Gdansk, Poland. From there, I had hoped to catch a ship on the Baltic Sea to Saint Petersburg, Russia. But rail restrictions in Bulgaria dictated otherwise and Gisela's invitation offered a desirable alternative, so I flew to Germany instead.

Gisela serves gourmet meals in her home and introduces me to friends at two dinner parties seasoned with laughter and intellectual conversation. We ride the *Alstershiffahrt*, the water taxi on Inner Lake Alster. "Hamburg has more canal miles than Venice," she says while dining at a stilt-supported, over-a-canal café.

Hamburg is a mecca for small watercraft: canoes, kayaks, rowboats, skulls, dragon boats, and sailing dinghies. The waterway can be so crowded that lessons and a license are required.

Earlier during my time in Germany, I had gone to Kassel, the city where my paternal great-grandparents were born and where I did ancestral research at the *stadtarchiv,* the city archives.

Above: Gisela van Riesenbeck (second from right) and her friends enjoy an evening of conversation and dining in Poppenbüttel. Below: The water taxi *Alstershiffahrt* on which we rode from Poppenbüttel into Hamburg, stopping at several taxi stations along the way.

During World War II, Kassel was a munitions center and, consequently, a target of Allied bombing that destroyed 90 percent of the city between 1942 and 1945. "That's why you don't see any older homes," says, Ursula, a very helpful archivist.

Kassel was also the home of Duke Wilhelm I, whose summer home was a huge, five-story neo-classic castle, Schloss Wilhelmshöhe, built in the late 1700s. This building, now an art gallery and museum, is so broad that I stand 300 meters from its columned entrance to encapsulate it in a wide-angle lens.

Facing the opposite direction, I use a telephoto to discern a copper statue of Hercules, 8.25 meters tall, that stands atop an octagonal base structure and pyramid—total height, 70.5 meters—on a hill 1.5 kilometers away.

This is Bergpark. With an area of 2.4 square kilometers, it's Europe's largest hillside park. Begun in 1696, it was not completed until the 1850s. The grass corridor between the castle and statue is the site of *wasserkükunste*, a once-a-month summertime event of water artistry that will occur later tonight.

The climb to Hercules takes an hour with stops for photos, conversations, and a beer and brat. Along the way, I drift into lush forests, cross stone aqueducts, and pass two ponds, a high-arched bridge, and a gray stone facade. The last 250 meters ascend parallel rock staircases on either side of a *kaskaden*, a series of cascading terraces that rises up from the upper edge of a third pond.

By dark at 10:00 pm, the hillside is covered with humanity. Some sit on benches and chairs at lower elevations. Some rest on blankets near the middle pond and bridge. And some stand at Hercules' feet. I and an English-speaking German couple I met here have chosen to be at the base of the upper pond.

"There, it's started," says Oliver, the German man, pointing up. The first liters of water drop about ten meters in a narrow stream as though being poured from an invisible cruet. People above descend the steps, racing the flow that cascades beside them. Brazen teens stand before the accelerating torrent, now wider, daring it to wet their feet. "They're the crazy ones," states Oliver.

Fifteen minutes later, the water has descended to our level, dropping the

Above: Looking up from the base of the *kaskaden*, people at *wasserküküunste* can see the statue of Hercules at the apex of the monument and watch water begin to flow downward. Right: The plume of pressurized water rises climactically at the pool. The Schloss Wilhelmshöhe is lit in the background, and a few city lights in Kassel are also visible. Below: Trams in Kassel promote the radio station BOB; with Bob being my nickname, I accept this as a personal welcome.

last ten meters into the upper pond and hiding a larger-than-life sculpture of Neptune who sits on a clamshell throne in an under-the-falls alcove. From there, the water goes out of sight, into a subterranean conduit.

"Let's go," says Oliver. "We've got 45 minutes." Having walked all the way up then down this hill earlier, in afternoon daylight, I figure we will need all of that, especially since we are now among thousands of others bent on the same purpose: to beat the water to the lower pond—in the dark.

We stop at the middle pond and bridge, where the water has already resurfaced again. Then, we stride on, purposely picking our steps on a packed dirt path. Passing grated manhole covers, we hear the water, thundering in an underground sluice beneath us, surging ever-downward.

Until it shoots up, that is. "There. There. Look." exclaims Oliver.

We are still 200 meters above the lower pond. Backlit from below, the plume rises and crests at 25 meters like a shape-shifting specter. At its upward-thrusting core, compressed droplets form a dark gray skeletal spine that stands erect then fragments into a twisted torso before falling away in a ghost-white diaphanous veil, dropping to the pond below. The plume gushes for 20 minutes, but even in its vanishing moments, it settles into demise gracefully, becoming less tall as the forces that had held it erect diminish.

Gravity, pressure, and gravity are the forces at play here. "No manmade pumps. No hydro engineering," Oliver confirms. Gravity initiated the hurtling stream up the hill where Hercules now stands alone. Pressure grew as the water channeled into a subterranean tube until bursting upward from a jet in the lower pond. Gravity, again, brought the graceful plume, droplet by droplet, back into equilibrium.

Gravity, meaning a serious subject, also sets the tone for conversation as I walk back to Kassel with three students at Universität Kassel. Phillip and Dominique from Germany and Chere from South Africa are studying global business, global education, and global economy, respectively. They plan to change the world, creating a platform for universal human equity.

These memories of landmarks and waterways flow through my mind as I, afloat again, travel from Germany to Russia. For three days, I am with truck drivers, motorcyclists, businessmen, and tourists aboard the cargo and passenger ferry *Translübeca* on our way from Lübeck to Sankt Petersburg.

I am grateful for the spectacles, monuments, and memorials. Yet, I am even more aware that these are merely backdrops for scenes enacted on the stage of local and world history. The conversations, hospitality, and friendships are the base currency for which I, a wayfaring traveler, am most grateful.

Chapter Five: Russia—Pushkin, Saint Petersburg, Moscow ... June 19 to July 2, 2010

Pushkin, a sister city of Kalamazoo, celebrated its 300th anniversary in June 2010 with festival, carnival, a parade, fireworks that were barely visible in mid-summer's White Night, and a solemn consecration of the community's cherished cathedral. The denizens were joined by dozens of international guests who rejoiced with them. I was among 20 who came from Kalamazoo.

Pushkin became a village in 1710, two years after Tsar Peter the Great gave the land to his wife Catherine I. Located 15 miles from St. Petersburg, which was then the Russian capitol, the site became known as Tsarskoye Selo (Tsar's Village). During the Communist Era, it was renamed Detskoye Selo (Children's Village). In 1937, Pushkin assumed its current name in concurrence with the 100th anniversary of the death of Russian poet Alexander Pushkin (1799 – 1837) who studied there in 1811.

During World War II, Catherine Palace and Alexander Palace, which were built by the royal family in the 1700s, were severely damaged but have since been restored to their original opulence and are open to the public. Similarly, St. Catherine Cathedral, a majestic five-domed Russian Orthodox edifice located in the village center, was rededicated in a solemn ceremony on Sunday, June 27, 2010, the last day of the Pushkin anniversary celebration.

Victor Afanasenko, director of the Pushkin Chamber of Commerce and Industry, explained that the cathedral was originally consecrated in 1840 then demolished 100 years later by the Bolsheviks who replaced it with a larger-than-life statue of Russian leader Vladimir Lenin. He added, "The statue mysteriously tumbled one night" in 2004 even though it weighed several tons and was located near the police station. Reconstruction of the cathedral began two years later.

A few hundred people were allowed inside for the six-hour rededication while thousands stood outside and countless others watched on television. Kalamazooan Garrylee McCormick was, very likely, the only American inside, an honor he attained by carrying to Pushkin three relics—a slice from the True Cross, a piece of the Blessed Virgin's veil, and a first-class relic (a bone particle) of St. Catherine—that were gifts from the Sisters of Saint Joseph and a former chaplain of the sister's convent in Nazareth, Michigan.

The reconstruction of these grand buildings—local and national treasures—were a tremendous source of pride for Pushkinites, including Larisa Boeva and her son, Slava, who took me into their home for eight days.

Larisa is an art teacher at a school for children with breathing disorders. She is also an accomplished artist and member of the Society of Pushkin Artists, which has links to Galesburg resident Jerolyn Selkirk, who was my entrée into the Boeva home.

St. Catherine Cathedral

Larisa Boeva and a self-portrait

Catherine Palace and Garden

Slava took me on a six-hour trek of the expansive Catherine Garden that surrounds Catherine Palace and Alexander Palace. Of his knowledge of local lore, he simply stated, "My mother and I walked here for as long as I can remember." Now at age 22 and having studied English in school, he patiently translated for Larisa and me as we shared our stories.

Twenty delegates of the Kalamazoo-Pushkin Partnership were on hand for the anniversary. Marie Stoline had recently written and published a book about residents of a home for retired Russian architects; she and her husband, Michael, delivered copies. Paul Asmus, traveling with his wife, Alice, donned a fake black beard and stovepipe hat to personify Abraham Lincoln. Jerolyn Selkirk and Betty Lee Ongley each took one of their college-age grandchildren. Frank Jamison, assisted by his wife, Paula, videographed the entourage and has since created a documentary.

I found special favor through invitations to people's homes. In Pushkin, one of Larisa's coworkers, Margarita Davuda, hosted a dinner party. Dancing about her kitchen, she suited me with an apron and announced that we were going to make dumplings.

Margarita Davuda (left) and her friend offer a toast to go with the dumplings we made.

In Saint Petersburg, Alesya Veter, a guide at a local sailing center who I met a month earlier in coastal Bulgaria, greeted me at the customs gate when I arrived by cargo ship from Germany and provided a tour of plazas and cathedrals. Sociology professor Dr. Leo Semashko, a client whose English writing I edit, hosted me for two days, including a celebration of his birthday. And Maria Gu, who I met at the festival, served dinner in her flat.

In Moscow, Marina Ilynikh, a Muscovite who spoke impeccable English and who I met in Barcelona seven weeks earlier, provided a grand tour. An engineer by profession, Marina calibrated our 14-hour day to include historical highlights, a therapeutic massage, and a side trip on the Metro to where I would catch a commuter train to Sheremetyevo Airport the next day.

Inside the Red Square Metro station, I noticed many people touching certain parts of bronze sculptures that typify proletariat workers, farmers, athletes, soldiers, schoolchildren, and others. Marina explained that a few years ago college students began to touch the sculptures as a prank. Today, people of all ages continue the practice—for good luck. The result is that some parts, such as dogs' muzzles, are now hand-polished to lustrous brilliance.

Above: A person walks quickly past the proletarian soldier's dog, reaching up with her right hand to get some luck from the dog's muzzle. Left: At the carnival in Pushkin, people demonstrate their culture, customs, and costumes. Below: Intercession Cathedral in Moscow. Next page: The oddly constructed Moskva Hotel. And the Tsar's Bell in the Kremlin; crafted in 1600, it weighs 40,000 pounds; it was dropped, broken, and never rung.

Near Red Square, the colorful Intercession Cathedral (also known as St. Basil's) is a religious anomaly. Built in the mid-1500s, it was not destroyed during the Communist Era. "It was planned to be blown up—after all, it was a church in Red Square—but for some reason it wasn't," Marina said.

She related that Red Square was originally a market and noted an expen-

sive department store nearby, but it has also been a military parade ground and a venue for major music concerts.

We strolled past Lenin's tomb, choosing not to wait in a long line there, but we did pause to observe sentries and an eternal flame at a World War II memorial.

Marina pointed to the Moskva (Moscow) Hotel and asked if I saw anything peculiar about it. Yes, the left wing comes forward while the right wing is flush with the center façade, and the windows are different from left to right. She explained that when the architect presented two sets of plans to Joseph Stalin, the Russian leader stamped his approval partly on both sets. Afraid to question, the architect built half of the building according to one set of plans and half according to the other. "Stalin was crazy. People were afraid of him," Marina explained.

Inside the Kremlin, Russia's seat of government, we found ornate office buildings, cannonry, suited politicians, and uniformed soldiers of various ranks—and a church and three cathedrals. Each was brilliantly topped with gold domes and crucifixes, and the interiors were rich with religious icons.

At the Temple to Christ the Savior, the world's tallest Russian Orthodox cathedral, Marina stated, "Throughout our history, when we conquered a country in battle, we built a church. This one was to honor the victory of Tsar Alexander I over Napoleon in 1812." She said the architects and builders couldn't find a site with solid footing, so they moved a pre-existing monastery. When

a worker fell and died, a nun cast a dubious curse on the building.

Completed in 1860, it was dynamited in 1931 by the Communists who intended to replace it with the Palace of the Soviets. But World War II and flooding of the nearby Moskva River prevented that project, so Nikita Khrushchev built the Moskva Pool, the world's largest outdoor swimming pool, there instead. In 1990, the Russian Orthodox Church received permission to rebuild the temple according to its original design. Begun in 1992, it was completed in 2000.

On a riverboat on the Moskva River, we floated past a 300-foot sculpture that features a large male figure in olden garb standing on the deck of and dwarfing an ancient sailing ship. Unveiled in 1997 by painter, sculptor, and architect Zurab Tsereteli, it has since been listed among the world's ugliest artistic creations. Marina said that Tsereteli crafted the sculpture with the likeness of Christopher Columbus and attempted to give it to New York City. When the U.S. refused the gift, he reshaped the head to that of Peter the Great.

Ten minutes downstream, we came upon a building, constructed in Russian Baroque and Gothic styles, that resembled a cathedral yet, because of its numerous rectangular windows, clearly was not. At the lower levels, its expansive wings looked like shoulders and arms that might encircle a courtyard. In the center, its tiers ascended to a multifaceted pinnacle about 30 stories tall. A 30-foot bronze sculpture at the base of the steeple depicted a proletariat couple holding a banner that bore the Russian Hammer and Sickle. And the spire, more than 100 feet tall, was crowned by the Communist Star and Wreath of Wheat insignia. With a smooth, sandstone façade and numerous spires, it portrayed practicality and prestige.

Marina said this was a residential building with 540 flats. Completed in 1952, it's one of seven similar Moscow structures nicknamed "Stalin's High-Rises" by Muscovites and "Seven Sisters" by others. Under the Communist regime, flats were given to workers for their service to the state. With Russia's current economy, however, many are occupied by children of the original recipients, often shared with siblings and their families. "People don't make enough money to buy a home, and even if mortgages are available, interest rates are 20 to 25 percent," Marina said.

Marina's special gift on this day was a visit to a museum that honors the writings and paintings of Nicholas Roerich who had traveled extensively in southern Russia, India, and China in the 1920s and 1930s. In particular, she wanted me to see a painting of a Himalayan *stupa* painted in rich blues and blacks as though lit by a full moon. The painting is called "Crossroads of Christ and Buddha," a title that expresses the belief that Jesus traveled the Silk Road during his "lost years" from ages 12 to 30.

Knowing that I would be in India among sacred places such as this on the next part of my journey, Marina stated, "Maybe their spirits will guide you." I replied that I was already being guided and blessed by many generous Russians who invited me into their homes, welcomed me to their celebrations, and opened their hearts to share their culture and communities.

Chapter Six: India's Magnetic Mystique ... July 2 to 28, 2010

India is a country of contrasts. Hand-drawn rickshaws parry with luxury autos. Plain-clad men straddle motorcycles while women in colorful saris ride sidesaddle behind them, perhaps cradling an infant in one arm. Children beg outside shopping malls. Earthly poverty shares space with spirituality.

Even India's geography is a contrast. Having stayed two weeks in Delhi, population 14 million, and two weeks in the Himalayas, I experienced a cacophony of constant car horns on crowded city streets and quiet majesty of wind-swept, snow-capped mountain peaks.

This is a typical traffic scene in Delhi: vehicles of all sorts tightly packed together; a motorcycle with three or more passengers, in this case, a helmeted male driver, a woman wearing a colorful sari and sitting side-saddle while cradling an infant in her left arm.

Indians say honking—they call it "horning"—is "a symphony in the streets." Foreigners say, "India assaults the senses." Both are correct. Those diverse perspectives define India's magnetic mystique. Of eight nations I visited in 2010, no other brought contrast so forcefully into my consciousness.

In Delhi, I was the guest of Rajat, a sports physician. My lodging was on the third floor of a brick-and-marble guesthouse with a realty office and a small tailor shop with elegant diaphanous, sequined dresses below. Across a narrow street rose a maze of one-room, honey-combed homes roofed with corrugated steel held down by rubble. I would call this a slum, but Rajat said it wasn't because the buildings were made of concrete rather than cardboard.

In the mountains, food served in roadside *dhabas* was prepared in woks heated by a single propane burner. The meals, generally curried rice, eggs, flatbread, and chai, were whatever the cook was making at the time.

Religion and spirituality were evident in urban temples, some prominent and others nested among alley homes. Islamic prayers that were broadcast from mosques on public address systems from dawn to night. In the mountains, robed lamas roamed village streets, monasteries clung to verdant cliffs, and roadside stupas were common. Caring showed in wizened women holding satin-skinned infants and a shepherd who carried his puppy sheepdog while moving his flock across a mountain road.

I wan to return. There's something about the place. For example ...

The Taj Mahal is an engineering marvel. Inscriptions from the Koran, carved in white marble then filled with black marble, border the arched entrances from a height of about eight to eighty feet; the characters gradually increase in size, with the larger at the top, giving the impression that all are the same height. Similarly, chevrons carved on columns create an illusion of facets that are not there.

Constructed without scaffolds in 1632 to 1647, this marble-and-jeweled mausoleum was built in five-foot increments with dirt piled next to previous levels to provide footing for workers as they erected the next five feet. When the mound was removed, the masterpiece emerged as a perfect equilateral octagon with a width that exactly matches the height of 180.5 feet.

Himalayan roads are built by hand, literally. The road crews, "handiworkers" as Rajat called them, are hardy mountain people who use ham-

Previous page bottom: Handiworkers toiling on the Leh-Manali Highway; they work at high elevations and great distances from towns, thus making the use of cement trucks impractical. Above: These two images also show why heavy machinery is seldom used; narrow roads with no guardrails and water that flows down mountainsides and across rocky, muddy roads.

mers to break rocks and shovels to mix concrete. Some road sections are fairly smooth, but washboard gravel or rutted mud is more common. Avalanches are frequent. Travel involves fording rocky streams. Lines of cars, trucks, and buses pass even on narrow curves and hairpin turns. There are no guardrails, and vehicles of errant drivers lie at the bottom of ravines hundreds of feet below.

Delhi traffic is a nearly constant snarl. Vehicles travel three to five abreast on what Americans would consider two-lane roads. The space between cars is minimal. Yet drivers have a keen sense of proximity not only to other motorized vehicles but also to pedestrians, bicycles, rickshaws, and cows who occupy the roadways.

With a population of 1.8 billion, India has a wealth of human resources and a challenge of finding work for them. Rajat employs two men to open the door for the dozen or so clients who visit his clinic daily.

On July 4, Rajat's housekeeper, Hari, taught me about independence. As I unloaded my backpack and put my clothes in a dresser, Hari stepped in front of me and, in halting English, proclaimed, "I do that!" and I realized I was infringing on his job. Daily, Hari prepared my meals, made my bed, cleaned the shower, and washed the floor. He was honored to have me there. My presence gave him purpose, and I learned to respect his responsibilities. When I left, he cried and said, "A sad day."

At KhardungLa, the world's highest motorable pass at 17,800 feet, Tashi, the military commander of a small outpost, helped me fly a kite I'd brought from America. Wearing spit-polished black boots, camouflage fatigues, and sunglasses, this middle-aged, handlebar-mustachioed soldier raced up a snow-covered slope with hand raised and kite fluttering. Then he invited me into his barracks for tea. Even though the date was mid July, it was warmed by a propane heater.

Large shops in the mountain village of Leh were the size of a single-car garage. The merchants, usually men, handled hardware: pickaxes, sledgehammers, oil pans, tin cups, keys. Small shops were the size of a walk-in closet. Those proprietors, primarily women, sold scarves, shawls, and jewelry.

In a comparably small open-air meat store, goat ribs hung unrefrigerated on hooks, flies buzzed about, and a lone butcher sat at a bench, cleaving pieces to order, wrapping the cuts in newspaper, then passing them through an unpaned window to customers on the streets. On sidewalks, itinerant vendors unfurled blankets and proffered plastic housewares, leather wallets, garden produce, and dried fruit and nuts. Signs for trekking services abounded. Everybody had something to sell.

In the Moti Market, I bought scarves from Rinchen who invited me into her shop. We sat on the floor. My right shoulder touched goods on one side, and her left shoulder touched goods on the other side; a cat could not have passed between us. She ordered tea from a nearby vendor. We talked of love marriages versus arranged marriages, of her two children and their education, of her rent, of health. We talked of human things.

Women of the Moti Market: Kunzes Dolma, Rinchen Dolma, and Sonam Palmo.

One week later on my second day back in the States, a flash flood roared through Leh. The Moti Market was wiped out. More than 200 people were killed. More were missing. Thousands were homeless. Food and water supplies were gone. The airport was closed. The clinic was damaged as was the Tibetan Children's Village I had visited.

I had gotten to know these people. Yes, I'll go back. There's something about the place.

India Again

Photo by Ivy Lim Meei Jiuan at Buddhist Main Temple, McleodGanj, India

In the previous series of stories, set in 2010, I had three destinations: Josep and Chus' wedding in Spain in May, the 300th anniversary celebration in Pushkin in June, and Le Ultra Ultramarathon in the Himalaya Mountains in July/ August. Rather than travel back and forth across the oceans and continents, I chose to combine them into one trip. Prior to leaving, I gave away my furniture, downsized for the fourth time in my life, and moved out of my apartment—a decision that generated a great feeling of freedom as I ventured forward into the global community.

Unlike my 2010 adventures with Rajat and others into the Himalayas, in 2011 I traveled alone. My journey began in Washington, D.C., at a ten-day Buddhist Kalachakra ceremony that featured the Dalai Lama in July. At the end of August, I attended teachings by His Holiness at the Buddhist Main Temple in McleodGanj, India. Then I returned to Leh—as promised in the previous story—to hopefully find the ladies of the Moti Market. From there, I visited other Himalayan cities, traveling by bus or car and driver. My ultimate destination was Kolkata (renamed Calcutta by the British) where I joined my friend and client Rosalie Giffoniello and helped her craft her memoir about educating the poor children in that city's over-crowded slums.

Dalai Lama Teaches Compassion

In his teachings, the Dalai Lama expresses his belief in "compassion for all sentient beings" from which "we develop respect, admiration, and freedom of gratitude." His Holiness delivers this message in numerous venues around the world, including at Buddhist initiation ceremonies called Kalachakra.

Kalachakra means "time wheel." The initiation honors all life cycles: cycles of nature, cycles of breath, and, according to the International Kalachakra Network, "the practice of controlling the most subtle energies within one's body on the path to enlightenment." Many of the people at the Kalachakra in D.C.—6,000 to 14,000, depending on the day—came to state or restate vows to Buddhist spiritual practices.

The Kalachakra ritual was initially taught by The Buddha 2,600 years ago. The initiation in D.C. was the 31st conducted by His Holiness, the current (Fourteenth) Dalai Lama, since 1954. The first two were in Tibet, many have been in India, and this was the fifth in the United States.

The program consisted of chanted prayers, dances, and ritual—with monks attired in red- and gold-brocade vestments—and His Holiness' teachings. A Long-Life Ceremony was part of a celebration for the Dalai Lama's 76th birthday on July 6.

A key visual component of the Kalachakra is the Full Body, Speech, and Mind Mandala, a temporary work of detailed art that denotes impermanence, a tenet of the Buddhist faith. The mandala is composed of individual grains of colored sand—white, red, black, green, yellow, and others—arranged to convey symbolism, including the individuality of all sentient beings. When dismantled on the last day, the colorful sands blend and become, collectively, gray, a representation of universal connectivity. The sand is then ceremoniously returned to nature—deposited in a nearby river—to depict the perfect peace of Kalachakra flowing in the everyday world.

I found the ceremony and grandeur of the Kalachakra to be an ironic contrast to the venue: the Verizon Center, a sterile, concrete sports arena with five levels of plastic seats, a huge, four-sided overhead monitor and two projection screens above the stage, and frigid air conditioning.

The Dalai Lama was accompanied by a few of his personal body guards, but security fell primarily to the U.S. State Department—and it was super-strict. To carry a camera into the arena, those of us in the media corps were required to arrive at a pre-announced time that varied from day to day. Our bodies and our bags were visually and electronically checked upon entrance. Then we assembled in a screening room and waited … and waited … and waited … until a K-9 handler and his German shepherd arrived to sniff our bags for bombs.

Then, we waited again to be escorted—in small groups—onto the main floor where the day's designated photo-op was occurring. We were given precisely five minutes to capture close-ups at the base of the main stage and another ten or fifteen minutes to capture long-shots from the sound booth at the far end of the main floor. Then we were escorted *completely* out of the building and were not allowed to return unless we came back sans cameras.

Of the ten days of the Kalachakra, I carried my camera three times, choosing on the other days to listen to His Holiness' wisdom, delivered with humor, from the media section on the arena's sixth level. For me, a few photos were enough but his message of compassion could go on forever.

At the teachings at the Buddhist Main Temple in McleodGanj, August 30 through September 1, His Holiness began with these words: "The purpose of this gathering is to achieve happy life, bountiful life. The proper way to achieve happy life, bountiful life, is … much development on the heart to the enlightened state. … With more compassion, you feel more people are friends."

The Dalai Lama applied this theme to the world's major religions, saying, "All teach love, compassion, forgiveness, tolerance, self discipline. These are the basis of moral ethics. … The real troublemaker is too much self-centered attitude. … You totally give yourself to God to reduce a self-centered attitude."

Left: The Dalai Lama sits on a throne at the Kalachakra initiation in Washington, D.C. A U.S. State Department agent stands in the foreground, his back turned to His Holiness, scanning the attendees for signs of violence. Right: The Dalai Lama walks through the Buddhist Main Temple in McleodGanj on his way to the room where he will offer his teachings of compassion. He is accompanied by Tibetan security personnel.

The environment of the teachings in Dharamsala was casual, with security provided by His Holiness' personal body guards and a few Indian army officers, some unarmed. Most of the 5,000 to 6,000 people in attendance sat semi-lotus fashion on colorful floor cushions. Everyone was close, a gelatinous mass that stretched and adjusted to accommodate neighborly requests to straighten legs.

While the majority of attendees dressed and expressed physical features of Tibetan Buddhists, many others, of various skin tone and countenance, also wore the attire and facial markings of Hindus, Jews, Muslims, Sikhs, and Christians. Tenzin Taklha, the Dalai Lama's joint secretary, said that approximately 35 nations were represented at the teachings.

Young monks passed through the crowd distributing tea and bread. At noon, they fed rice, dal, and chai tea to everyone who brought their own bowl and spoon. Elders sat and children roamed freely yet silently in a tent-covered courtyard. Those outside the tent scurried in when monsoon rains made their daily appearance.

The Dalai Lama spoke primarily in Tibetan, his words carried over loudspeakers. Translators who spoke English, Spanish, Korean, and other languages sat with microphones among the crowd, and their words were broadcast over FM frequencies to which people listened through ear phones attached to radios, iPhones, and iPods.

On my first day, I sat on a mat, cozily close to others, and slightly out of sight of the Dalai Lama. The Spanish translator was four people to my left, her voice soft but audible. For the second and third days, I chose the courtyard, leaning against a tree, with room to stretch my legs and an umbrella close at hand.

In all, it was an idyllic mountain setting. No matter where I sat or roamed, I felt kinship among these people.

During my two brief encounters with the Dalai Lama, I have observed his uncanny ability to make strong eye contact. The first time was at a PeaceJam conference in Denver, Colorado, in 1996. Here, he looks straight into my eyes and camera lens as he enters a platform over the Anacostia River near Washington, D.C. for the Kalachakra dissolution ceremony in which grains of sand from the Full Body, Speech, Mind Mandala are returned to nature.

What Is Tibet? Who Are Tibetans?

Larger than Western Europe, the nation of Tibet is home to six million people. Known as "the roof of the world," the country has an *average* elevation of 13,000 feet. Five of Asia's great rivers originate in Tibet, and nearly half of the world's population lives downstream.

The history of Tibet and Tibetan Buddhism includes political and spiritual association with the Manchurians, the Mongols, and historical figures such as Genghis Khan. Yet, today, Tibet is not recognized as a nation by the world's political powers.

In 1949, the People's Liberation Army of Communist China invaded Tibet. After negotiations with the Chinese leader Mao Tse Tung failed, the Dalai Lama fled from his palatial home in Lhasa, Tibet, to McleodGanj, India, in 1959.

The Tibetan Government-in-Exile, located in nearby Dharamsala, is comprised of democratically elected legislative, judicial, and executive bodies. Tibetan Buddhism teaches how to achieve deep and abiding happiness, free from suffering, with an emphasis on spiritual rather than material development.

Numerous non-government organizations, many of them headquartered in Dharamsala, strive to keep the Tibetan identity alive. But perhaps the most outstanding endeavors are being done by Tibetan Children's Villages. Having started in one location with 51 students in 1960, TCV now houses and provides quality education to 17,000 young people—some of them orphans—at 20 schools in India.

The following poem, crafted by a TCV student and published in the recent TCV newsletter, captures the essence of the questions: What is Tibet? Who are Tibetans?

Identity of a Tibetan

By Tenzin Namdhak
Level 10 student at Tibetan Children's Village

Thank you, shae shae, and mercy
English, Japanese and French
Known around the world
But what is our identity?

A tourist seated next to me
Curiously he asked, are you Nepali?
No, are you Sherpa? No, are you Ladakhi?
No, he kept on his queries, but I answered no, no ……

At last exhausted, he revealed his last query
Then who are you?
Immediately, I answered to him
I am a Tibetan.

The man seemed to be in a dilemma
With a heap of question
But he was totally sure
That he hadn't heard this name before.

Let us raise our voice
And reveal our story against
The Red empires choice
Among the people of this world.

Reprinted with permission from "Metok: A Newsletter from the Tibetan Children's Villages." Summer, 2011. Vol. XLIX

Photos below and top of next page: Children and the director of the Upper Tibetan Children's Village school near Dharamsala. Next page center: Children and elders at the Tibetan Children's Village near Leh in the region of Ladakh. Next page bottom: An elder Lama walking the crowded streets of Leh and Gompa, a young enthusiastic Tibetan Buddhist monk in Dharamsala.

On August 8, 2011, the Dalai Lama relinquished half of his dual role as both the spiritual and temporal leader of the Tibetan people by turning the temporal responsibility over to Lobsang Sangay, who was democratically elected to fill that position by Tibetans around the world.

On the surface, this is a practical political move for a man of 76 who is much in demand to speak about Buddhist compassion and world peace. Yet, the action impacts a 350-year tradition.

In 1653, the Great Fifth Dalai Lama was the first to become the spiritual and temporal leader of the Buddhist Tibetan people. Every Dalai Lama since, including this one, the Fourteenth Dalai Lama, has held this theocratic power. However, this change confirms His Holiness' belief that restoring a purely spiritual role to the office of the Dalai Lama will "benefit Tibetans in the long run."

The Women in the Moti Market

Rinchen Dolma, Sonam Palmo, and Kunzes Dolma are sitting in front of their shops in Leh, India's Moti Market as I approach. They're chatting, smiling, and laughing—just as they were when I first met them. They recognize me within seconds even though it's been a little more than a year since we last saw each other. Rinchen rises from her chair and reaches out to greet me. "You want chai?" Sure that I'll accept her offer, she runs to get some from a nearby tea shop.

The gathering of neighboring shop owners grows to six women and a child clustered in front of these series of shops that are tiny by Western standards. Kunzes' and Sonam's stores are smaller than a single-car garage, and Rinchen's is about the size of a walk-in closet. They sell cloth goods of one sort or another.

Last year, Rinchen and I engaged in significant conversation on subjects of love marriage versus arranged marriage, family, health, education, and commerce. She gladly reports that her migraine headaches are gone and she no longer travels to Delhi for treatment. Her teenage son is now studying communication in a boarding school in southern India; supported by a wealthy benefactor, he will likely complete his formal education in a different nation. Prepared for that eventuality, Rinchen proudly produces her recently acquired passport. On her digital camera, she shows me photo after photo of her blossoming 10-year-old daughter.

This reunion is especially gratifying for me because one week after I got to know these delightful women in late July 2010, I heard inadequate news reports of a devastating killer flood in Leh. Not able to contact them, I wondered, "Are they all right?" I've come back to find out.

They are. "The flood was down there," says Kunzes, dismissively gesturing toward a lower elevation closer to the nearby Indus River. Then we turn our attention to the photos I had taken last year and brought with me now. They're delighted to receive them.

Also okay are Tsewang, another shopkeeper who sells children's clothing a few meters away, the Tibetan proprietors of Montessori Restaurant with whom I had conversations about the Dalai Lama, and the young family of wallet vendors who daily spread their wares on a blanket on the curb of a busy street. All of these were glad to have these photos; the family gave me a 25 percent discount on a wallet in appreciation.

The only tragic news comes from Kelsang, the cousin of Tseten, a jeweler I had met in another part of Leh. "She's no longer with us," Kelsang states. "She died giving birth in April. An infection, and they didn't have money to treat it. The child is alive." Kelsang, who now owns and runs the tiny 6-foot by 6-foot shop, holds back tears as I give her photos of Tseten I had taken last year.

Left column: Rinchen Dolma and I sit on the floor of her tiny shop. Above: Kunzes Dolma and Sonam Palmo. Below: Our reunion one year after the other photos were taken.

Others in the Moti Market

On various days, I roamed the streets of Leh, primarily the Moti Market with its entrance marked by two white *stupas* and a line of Buddhist prayer wheels. Each time, I was captivated by the people, the sounds, and the opportunity to capture images of the culture, especially closeups of facial expressions.

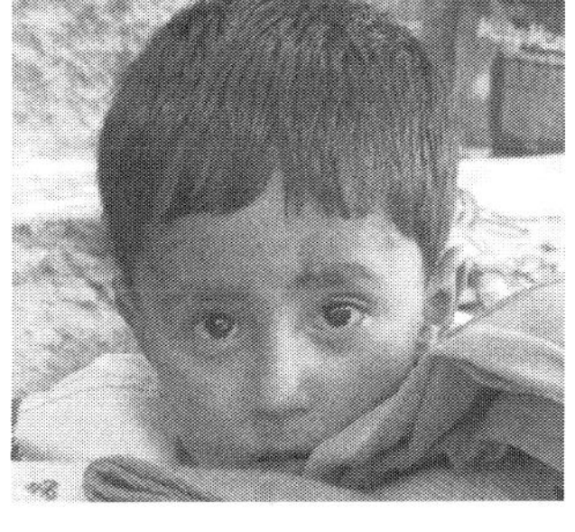

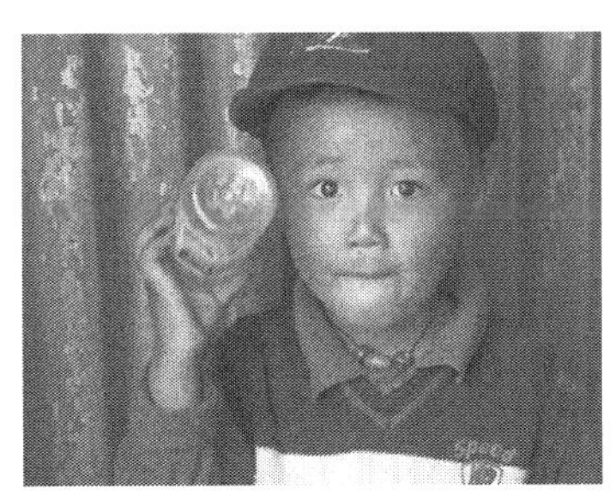

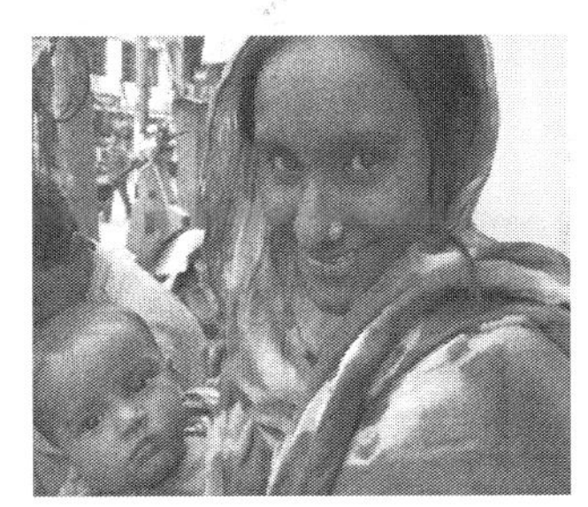

Rebuilding Homes and Lives in Ladakh, India

"I'd rather be 100 percent responsible for a small job than two percent responsible for a big job," states Rachit Srivastav, a 23-year-old graduate from an architectural college in Delhi.

Rachit, "not wanting a corporate job," is working, instead, high in the Himalayas in the northern Indian region of Ladakh. Here, as a member of the non-governmental organization Architects Without Borders, he's helping Ladakhis rebuild their homes after a killer flood roared through these mountains on August 6, 2010.

The flood was not typical, the result of a swollen river that rises slowly and gives people fair warning. No, this flood originated with a cloudburst that thundered down from higher elevations.

Official estimates of downpour volume vary widely from one-half inch to nearly ten inches in a region that gets an average of six-tenths rainfall during the month of August—and it all fell within one-half hour from 1:30 to 2:00 in the middle of the night. "The rain washed down water channels formed by glaciers or humans toward the Indus River," catching people asleep and unaware, Rachit explains.

The death toll was set at a little over 200 people with more than that missing. "They don't know how many bodies were washed away," says a mountain climber who was there.

Katherine Johnson, an Architects Without Borders volunteer, was trekking and caught in the storm. She, her companions, and their guide dealt with hypothermia, sodden terrain, and roaring rivers in which she and a friend nearly drowned.

Rebuilding in the aftermath in remote regions is a major task. So, when Rachit labels his managerial work here in Ladakh as "a small project," he's referring to the size of the homes. Constructed by skilled Nepalese masons and local Ladakhi laborers, these are one-room structures, about 20 feet by 20 feet, in which many family members might live.

Yet, Rachit's work and that of others who oversee the project is far from small. In volume, the Architects Without Borders people are constructing eight homes and two public shelters at five job sites. Rachit's goal is to build 25 to 30 homes. Managing the labor force is a tremendous growth experience for this young man. At two sites, the masons protest their wages, and Rachit engages them in lengthy conversation before resolving the issue—at least for now.

Administration of funds to both the contracted laborers and the homeowners is the work of Amita Shanbhogue, a 27-year-old volunteer with the NGO SEEDS India. "We pay the contractors 110,000 rupees ($2,400 U.S.) for the labor," she states. "This is more than normal because the homes are in the mountains." Here, the views are spectacular, but the work is devoid of social life and, to the workers, deserving of higher wages.

In addition, SEEDS gives the beneficiaries 300,000 rupees ($6,500 U.S.) to buy construction materials. "If they spend more, they have to pay it themselves," Amita adds, "so I help them manage their money and be careful with material selection and cost."

At one site, Amita, an Indian who works for Deloitte Consulting in Philadelphia, Pennsylvania, gives one of seven weekly installments to a beneficiary. The elderly Indian is illiterate and marks the receipt with an inked thumb impression. "This is common and all the banks accept it as his signature," she explains.

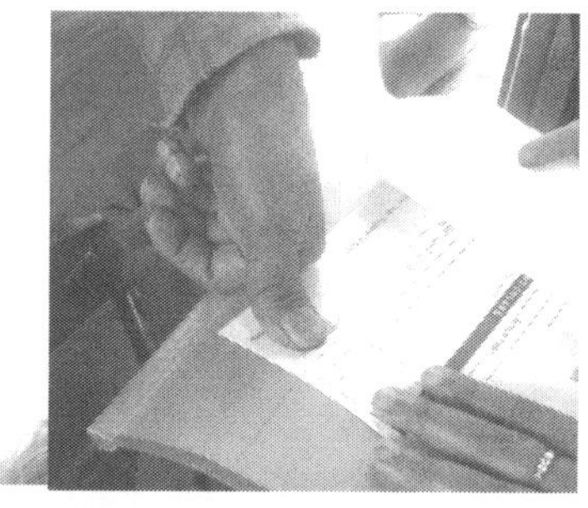

Many of the destroyed homes and businesses were between Leh and nearby Choglamsar where a Tibetan Children's Villages (TCV) is located. Sonam, an administrator there, says that educational roles were set aside for four weeks after the flood as elders, adults, and children took in displaced neighbors.

Some of the homeless were Tibetans who (or whose parents) had migrated from Tibet when the Chinese invaded that nation in the 1950s. Many others were Ladakhis, thus creating a beautiful irony of Tibetans, who were once immigrants themselves, taking in Ladakhis who had helped them and their families decades earlier.

Of people who required medical assistance, Sonam adds, "We treated them at our clinic for three or four days. Then they were taken to the hospital in Leh."

This spirit of cooperation typifies the ongoing endeavors of Ladakhis and Tibetans to maintain their distinct cultures in an amalgamated society where winter temperatures reach –30 Celsius and environmental conditions necessitate cooperation.

This spirit of identity and blending are also visible in the homes being funded by SEEDS India and designed by Architects Without Borders.

The principle building material is mud bricks covered with mud plaster inside and out. The roofs are made of poplar beams and twigs from the local *talu* tree, covered with grass and clay. "The grass is for insulation and the clay for waterproofing," Rachit explains, "and it breathes," which is beneficial for properly venting the dung-burning *bukhari* stoves, set in the middle of the room, for winter heat.

At the same time, these young, educated professionals bring technological innovations that are acceptable to the locals. "We want to give them earthquake safety, flood safety, and passive solar thermal heat," Rachit states.

Earthquake safety comes from buttressed corners that are not typical of Ladakhi homes. "The corner is the weakest point. When the corner gives, the wall falls, and the ceiling collapses. That's the major cause of death in an earthquake," Rachit explains.

Flood safety is provided by a building technique known as "seismic bands," which are connected pieces of wood that surround the building above the foundation and below the ceiling plate. The concept is the same as encasing boxes on a pallet with shrink-wrap plastic prior to shipping.

Thermal insulation is the result of walls up to two feet thick, a technique that the Ladakhis have used for centuries. However, the architects are teaching the locals to paint the southern exposure black and then install a sheet of glass two inches away from the exterior surface. "This creates a greenhouse effect," says Rachit. "The sun's heat is trapped during the daytime then radiates through the wall to warm the house at night."

One morning, Toby Pear, an architectural volunteer from England, talks about going home soon. "My mum will be happy if I'm there for Christmas," he says. That night, his face is reddened from exposure to high-altitude sun while working on the community shelter projects. "It looks like I've wangled myself a job back here again next year," he says with cockney spirit. His smile is unusually broad. "I can't think of a better place to work."

This home at the first of four sites we visited features wide double buttresses at each of its four corners, a seismic band at the base and near the top of the buttresses, thick walls, a southern-facing wall that is painted black and will be covered with windows to gather solar heat.

This column of photos shows a home under construction in a beautiful Himalayan valley where workers want more money because of its remote location; the homeowner serving naan and chai tea to us; Rachit, the homeowner, I, and our driver pose (photo by Amita Shanbhogue); and a yak on a stone-lined path.

International Movies Come to Calcutta

The World Comes Home.
8 days. 50 countries. 125 directors. 150 films.

Thus reads the promotional material for the Seventeenth Kolkata Film Festival, 10 –17 November 2011, one of the world's most renowned cinema events. An exciting gala from the opening ceremony to the last flicker of credits.

The movies, mostly feature-length with a few shorts, were shown in 11 venues across the city, making them easily accessible to Kolkatans and international guests. More than 2,600 delegates, who paid an entry fee of 300 rupees ($6.00) each, as well as numerous media with complementary press passes attended. One hundred fifty films, representing the work of 125 directors from 50 nations, were shown.

The premier viewing location was Nandan-West Bengal Film Centre, Kolkata's showcase for cinema that includes five theaters, including one of the city's most popular.

The Kolkata Film Festival, which is accredited by the International Federation of Film Producers Association, Paris, is the second oldest film festival in India with the oldest being the International Film Festival of India that started in 1952. This one in Kolkata started in 1995 thanks to the work of Indian master filmmakers Satyajit Ray, Mrinal Sen, and Ritwik Ghatak. The festival was an inevitable result of the West Bengal government's establishment of Nandan in 1985, a move advocated by Ray, who was the film centre's first chair.

The Nandan location also featured an extensive exhibit of still photographs by Satyajit Ray from the 1950s and 1960s. Ray, who was born in Kolkata in 1921, received a posthumous Special Oscar Award from the US Academy of Motion Pictures in 1992, the year of his death, for his lifetime achievements in filmmaking. He was the first Indian to be so honored. Ray's son and the man behind the exhibit, Sandip Ray, said the photos in this exhibit were taken by his father during location hunting and at film festivals around the globe.

The opening ceremony for the Kolkata Film Festival was attended by thousands who thunderously applauded Shah Rukh Khan, a superstar actor of Bollywood, which is the informal name for the extensive film industry in Mumbai (Bombay), India. The opening ceremony also featured a screening of *The Magicians*, a terrific 93-minute film produced in The Netherlands and directed by Joram Lürsen.

Many of the films shown here were produced in India and other Asian nations. Quite a few came from the Middle East, Europe, and Central and South America. There were a handful from the United Kingdom and only two from the United States. Talk among the attendees indicated that the best movies came from Iraq, Iran, and Eastern Europe. Most were either in English or had English subtitles.

These movies were not of the Hollywood variety. Happy endings were not guaranteed. Fast-action and explosive stunts were not the norm. Fluff was not to be found. Some of the plots were exquisite while the storyline in a few might only be appreciated by people of the cultures from which the film originated. Many were truly works of art with long scenes that allowed viewers to appreciate the cinematographic beauty much as one might enjoy gazing upon a masterpiece in a museum or a lingering sunset.

In short, the Kolkata Film Festival was a grand smorgasbord of movies like the world-class independent and foreign movies shown by the Kalamazoo Film Society on the Western Michigan University campus but in a multi-theater venue amplified and multiplied thousands of times over to achieve a grand and dynamic scale.

The Movies I Saw

The Magicians (Netherlands, 2010) is a delightful, humorous, touching story about a bumbling tree surgeon who keeps falling out of trees and his young son, both of whom decide to become magicians. Starting with small audiences, they work their skills up to professional standards with the son showing great proficiency at prestidigitation and the father providing comic relief. When the father makes their young female assistant disappear … and can't bring her back, the story line elevates to a touching display of family togetherness in the face of adversity. All thumbs up; see it if you can.

Once Upon a Time in Anatolia (Turkey, 2011) is a cinematographic work of art with a slice of life storyline of a police murder investigation. Filmed at night and in other low-light settings, the gorgeous scenes are illuminated by automobile headlights, oil lamps, moonlight, and bonfires. A very slow-paced movie with intense close-up cinematography, this movie takes its time to reveal the personal lives of the police investigator, medical examiner, suspect, and victim. Two thumbs up … if they don't tire of the slow pace.

Black Rain (Japan, 1989) captures the human horror of Hiroshima in the minutes, hours, and years after its obliteration by an atomic bomb on August 6, 1945. The principal characters—a husband, wife, and their niece—face physical and emotional pain from radiation poisoning, "the black rain." After premature deaths of the wife/aunt and niece, director Sohei Imamura delivers his poignant punch line. Listening to a news report about the United States potentially dropping an atomic bomb to end the Korean War, the husband/uncle says, "Humans never learn. They strangle themselves." Two thumbs up.

The Sound of Noise (Sweden, 2010) is a quirky, high-energy flick with a delightfully strange storyline. The principal roles are a male police detective, born tone-deaf into a family of world-class orchestral musicians, and a radical female percussionist who orchestrates a series of musical crimes perpetrated by six drummers. Through plot twists and slapstick, these characters on opposite sides of the law team up to help the detective overcome his loathing of musical sound. Two thumbs up.

Uncle Boonmee who can recall his Past Lives (Thailand, 2010) is mis-titled. Uncle Boonmee doesn't recall his past lives, but he is visited by the spirit of his deceased wife and his son who, though alive, is now a black-haired, red-eyed monkey ghost. The most distinguishing feature of this film are interminable scenes with no action, such as three people sitting on a bed watching television. Thumbs are not even twitching.

Beloved (France, 2011) is a dud with a storyline but no plot, sex but no love, and characters without character. It started out cute with the song "These Boots Are Made for Walking" in French but even cinema icon Catherine Deneuve, clothed or not, couldn't move the dreadful plot beyond that. Two thumbs down (although many in the packed house applauded).

Flamenco Flamenco (Spain, 2010) is a delight of artistry and dance with dramatic lighting and dynamic shadows set with a backdrop of fine art. The movie features the human body's amazing ability to generate tunes, thrum piano keys, finger-pick Spanish guitars, clap sophisticated syncopation, and tap dance with grace and flare. Age is irrelevant in *Flamenco Flamenco* as it ends with a chorus of youth and granddames and gray-haired gentlemen performing with pure heart. At least two thumbs up.

Raju (Germany and India, 2010) is a 24-minute short about a German couple who come to Kolkata to adopt an orphan son. While still in India, the couple learn the boy had been stolen from his family by a crime syndicate fronted by an "orphanage." In a post-screening interview, actress Taranjit Kaur, who played the orphanage director, said such kidnappings still occur in Kolkata with the children sold either to clueless foreign families or into a world of sex trafficking. Two thumbs up.

Rosalie Giffoniello Empowers Calcutta's Children

Rosalie Giffoniello holds a young boy at Preyrona 2 School in Kolkata (Calcutta). The boy has just received a new shirt and shorts prior to the Hindu holiday of Durga Puja. The clothes are courtesy of donations from Rosalie's nonprofit organization Empower the Children.

In Calcutta, India, the population density is nearly 25,000 people per square kilometer. To visualize that, imagine everyone in Portage (pop. 45,000) residing and working in the square mile bounded by Westnedge, Milham, Oakland, and Romence.

In a single-classroom, student populations of 60 or 70 are common. For another visual, imagine that many young people, ages 3 to 19, sitting on the floor of your two-car garage, learning from two or three teachers who are presenting different subjects, perhaps in different languages, at the same time.

This is the environment into which Rosalie Giffoniello, a retired special educator from New Jersey, co-founded the organization Empower The Children. It is through Rosalie that I, from September 2010 into January 2011, came to witness the unimaginable in education—and to observe what she and others like her, Indians and involved internationals, are doing to raise learning standards there.

During that time and for the next two years, I worked with Rosalie in Calcutta (the indigenous spelling is Kolkata) and helped her craft her memoir about her work in Calcutta: *Reclaiming Lives: Rediscovering Myself While Helping Kolkata's Poor.*

In 1999, recently divorced and striving to overcome fears of traveling alone, Rosalie, then 53, found structure by volunteering for a summer at Daya Dan, Mother Teresa's orphanage for disabled children in Calcutta. She worked with more-abled boys, preschool to early teens, who had some potential for independent living. Then, in January 2000, she took an early retirement from teaching in the U.S. and returned to Daya Dan for most of the next two years.

She taught the Sisters of the Missionaries of Charity and other volunteers to implement interactive language programs she had honed over 28 years of teaching in New Jersey, plus programs to help the children feed, dress, and bathe themselves. She and the Sister-in-Charge at Daya Dan were instrumental in getting a blind child accepted into a school for the blind and, later, a few others into a private special education school.

And Rosalie, who has no biological children of her own, became hooked on doing this work—and more—in Calcutta.

She recalls one day at a Missionaries of Charity function when the Dalai Lama clasped her hands and thanked her for "devoting your life to these children." In truth, Rosalie admits to feeling a sense of panic over His Holiness' words. She wanted to blurt, "My *whole* life? Or just the rest of my ten-year visa? My whole life is an awfully long time!"

Yet, it appears that Rosalie, now 65 and into the first year of her second ten-year visa, is on a lifetime path of service to Calcutta's poor.

She works under the auspices of Empower The Children, a 501(c)3 nonprofit that she and Janet Grosshandler, also of New Jersey, co-founded in 2001. Originally ETC's purpose was to raise funds for Daya Dan, but their focus soon grew to also work with and fund teachers at "non-formal schools" that offer classes and give exams but are not recognized as official "formal schools" by the Indian government. The quality of education in the ETC-sponsored schools is such that, when a student transfers into a government school, he or she is generally at the head of the class.

Rosalie's first educational experience outside Daya Day was in conjunction with one woman, Reena Das, and a group of students who met for one hour each day—during Reena's lunch hour from her duties as office manager for an architectural firm. The children were homeless street urchins. Classes included a healthy snack and introduction to the Bengali and English alphabets. The "classroom" was the steps of the office building where Reena worked then, later, the roof where the children ran about—dangerously close to the edge, in Rosalie's opinion—joyously viewing their world in a way they never could from the streets.

By July 2003, all of Rosalie's educational efforts and ETC's money became channeled toward an orphanage for boys, a non-formal school for the disadvantaged, a home for mentally disabled young adults, a hospital that performs free orthopedic corrective surgery for children and infants, and a tutorial center for teenage girls. On January 26, 2006, Rosalie and Reena opened the first school totally under the auspices of ETC. Reena named it Preyrona, which means "inspiration." Within five months, came Preyrona 2 School, then Preyrona 3 School in 2009.

This latter school originated as a clean three-story structure with adequate teaching space purchased with funds from Reena's uncle. But the predecessors, Preyrona 1 and Preyrona 2, are stories of the rising phoenix.

Preyrona 1 was originally located inside a single-room slum building that a men's group used at night as a *chaupal,* a community clubhouse, to gossip and smoke. After renting there four years, Rosalie and Reena moved the school to a more-modern, two-story building dedicated solely to vocational education, including sewing instruction for teenage girls and neighborhood women.

Preyrona 2 is a deplorable one-room building, 24 feet by 24 feet with no windows, chafed walls, a leaky roof that drips monsoon rain on the children, two decrepit ceiling fans, and unsafe electrical wiring. Yet, for the 90 students who attend there, it's better than no school at all.

Fortunately, at the time this article goes to press, Preyrona 2 is being demolished, soon to be replaced by a very modern—by Calcutta's standards—three-story building that will allow for expanded educational and vocational programs. Funding is being provided by Empower The Children and organizations in The Netherlands and Japan.

Some of the 90 children who attend the original Preyrona 2 School sit on the floor in their new holiday clothes.

Much credit goes to Ashit Sur, Reena's son, who toils tirelessly in all three of the Preyrona schools to make sure the children have a nutritional hot meal each day and the best education possible under the circumstances. For the demolition and replacement of Preyrona 2, he has worked diligently with government officials, contractors, and slum neighbors who live within arm's reach of the school.

One woman conquers fear to help children rise above poverty.

Today, in Calcutta, Rosalie teaches lessons at the Preyrona schools, the orthopedic hospital, and the home for mentally challenged adults. She personally helps deliver new holiday clothing to all ETC schools. When not in India, usually six months per year, she gives speeches and raises funds in New Jersey, New York, Pennsylvania, California, and Scotland. In March 2011, she spoke to St. Michael Lutheran Women's Fellowship in Portage on the same night that I gave a presentation there on reconstructed churches in Russia.

Rosalie's teaching methodology is self-empowering and love-giving. "Happy children become smart children. That's why we give the children only love," she says.

In a nation where educators still discipline with a switch, this is a challenge for some teachers. "When I interview a teacher, I explain that any form of violence is strictly prohibited and will lead to immediate dismissal," Rosalie adds. "I tell them, 'If you love the children, then they'll work for you. They'll want to please you and make you proud. It's our responsibility to give them the *right kind* of attention.'"

With that attitude, vibrant enthusiasm, an ever-present smile, and generous donations from people in many nations, Rosalie and Empower The Children bring hope to hundreds of children, young adults, and women who, otherwise, would not likely receive any education at all.

"If you love the children, then they'll work for you. They'll want to please you and make you proud."

Rosalie's book chronicles the accomplishments of Empower The Children, but—more importantly—it demonstrates what a woman at mid-life can do when she replaces fear with love and dares to adventure into the larger world of helping others, especially the part of the world where life for slum children often leads to begging, drugs, early marriage and premature pregnancy, or involvement in sex trafficking. *Reclaiming Lives* is available on Amazon.com.

Rosalie is now in her 12th year in Calcutta. Empower The Children, in its 10th year of operation, continues to donate funds for some combination of teachers' salaries, clothing and hot meals for children, supplies, and sponsorship of cultural drama, dance, and art programs in 11 different institutions.

One former ETC girl has graduated from college, another girl is now attending college, and a boy is enrolling in the spring. Fifteen women have taken the Usha Sewing Machine examination and will receive tailoring certification.

Through these efforts, children and women are rising out of poverty and enabling themselves to take advantage of India's booming economy and employment opportunities. Thus, they are gaining greater respect within their families and community.

The Philippines

Huge City, Remote Beach

The monsoon is dropping a deluge on Manila. The taxi driver says roads might be flooded, so he takes an alternate route from the airport. We drive for more than hour past buildings that all look the same, and it seems as though this city of 11.5 million people will go on forever. Why didn't I just book a room in a nice hotel?

Fortunately, the driver, Romulo, is of good spirits and pleasant conversation. He says that he and his family live near my destination, and he invites me to visit. Sure, I say. "We live in a squatter's neighborhood," he adds. "Nobody owns their homes. We've been there 20 years."

After 90 minutes, we arrive at the NGO headquarters where I'm to stay for the next three days. In the rain and near darkness, it's small sign is hidden behind huge palm fronds. It's a good thing that Romulo knows the neighborhood; another taxi driver might not have found this place.

Rey, the NGO manager, greets us. I've already told Romulo to wait—just in case. But the room is nice, clean, albeit small, and it'll do just fine. So he totes my backpack while I carry my smaller pack with computer, camera, and other precious devices.

Over breakfast the next morning, Rey and I engage in the first of several conversations about his NGO, the Philippine Partnership for the Development of Human Resources in Rural Areas (PhilDHRRA), and its mission to empower rural communities toward sustainable development.

On my second day there, I visit Romulo. His wife, Shirley, and elder son, Patrick, meet me at the edge of their neighborhood, and we stand under the steps of a pedestrian overpass to avoid rain. Romulo is late coming home from working a ten-hour shift. He's not allowed to drive the taxi home, so he commutes by *jitney*, which are small buses patterned after World War II general purpose vehicles (Jeeps), for two or more hours each way. On the night he drove me to PhilDHRRA, he arrived back at the airport very late and slept on a bench there.

When Romulo arrives, we walk along an alley where vendors sell domestic goods, toys, and food that ranges from fruit to fish. Their home has three rooms. We sit on a wooden bench and three plastic lawn chairs in the main room; it's, about 15 by 15, L-shaped, with a cooking area to the rear. A television, powered by a bright orange drop cord, stands on a small table a few feet from my knees. The second room is barely big enough for a cot. The third room is upstairs, accessed by a concrete stairway.

We talk for an hour, sharing stories of our lives. Patrick and his brother are in college, and Jessa, the daughter, is in high school; she has a Facebook page. Romulo earns 300 pesos a day. The sons' tuition is 5,800 pesos per trimester. When there's not enough money, the family borrows from a neighborhood cooperative because interest on a bank loan is outlandish. Romulo's sister lives there full time, and Shirley's sister is visiting for a few months while receiving medical treatment.

We listen and laugh. These are happy people, thankful for their family love and the friendly neighborhood in which they live. They recognize that the Western world is more affluent, but they seem to feel no disadvantage nor hold any disregard.

Rey and I also enjoy in-depth talks about the work of his NGO, part of a network of 67 NGOs to foster agrarian self-reliance in The Philippines. The building in which I'm staying provides lodging for transient students and researchers who come to nearby Loyola University.

I'm welcome to return there in January, Rey insists, but my heart is set on some dreamy South Pacific island. I ask Rey, "Where?" and he recommends Bohol, the island of his birth, and its sister resort island, Panglao.

So, at the airport while waiting for my outbound flight to Delhi, I book a round trip flight from Manila to Bohol for a week when I'll pass back through here six months hence.

I time the flights so I won't need to leave the Manila airport. But later, while in Kolkata, Philippine Air changes their schedule; so, in January, I stay overnight at one of those nice hotels near the airport, courtesy of the airline. At that hotel, a clerk recommends an economical guesthouse near the beach in Panglao with nice rooms, A/C, an outdoor pool, and a full breakfast for $40 a night.

Panglao is one of those picture-perfect places that people in snowy climes pine for during the depth of winter.

I take a holiday. No computer. No Internet. Camera used only twice. No trying to visit natives' homes. Minimal interaction with tourists.

Let's face it. Kolkata was crowded, noisy, dirty. Never before have I slept to the sounds of strangers' voices. Never before have I cleaned my fingernails *daily* because of dust in the air. Never had my body perspired so extensively even without exertion. And judging from what I saw of Manila, that city is huge too.

Here, white beach sand slopes to the water's edge, waves gently lick the shore, the water is delightfully warm and clear. Dozens of colorful outriggers, most named after Christian saints, ride peacefully on moorings while captains await tourists who want transportation to dolphin areas and snorkeling sites. I walk, wade, swim, rest … walk, wade, swim, rest … walk, wade, swim, rest ...

Cadres of women in professional medical attire roam the beach, offering massage. I accept … one per day. The therapist unfolds a sheet and lays it on the sand. I stretch out and squirm until the sand conforms to my body. And she begins. The oil applications are ample, and my skin drinks it in. Sand grit is a perfect exfoliant, and my skin sheds Kolkata residue.

As the sun sets, beach-side restaurants open for evening fare. People eat with bare feet in the sand. Native flame twirlers and celestial bodies, uninhibited by light pollution, entertain. I eat fresh fish, crab, and lobster self-served buffet-style straight off the grill.

I invest a day on an outrigger, beginning before sunrise. We spot dolphins, eat breakfast on a remote island, snorkel, drink coconut water on a spit of land that submerges as the tide rises. Star fish pose motionless on white sand beneath the water, their shapes convoluted by gentle rippling waves.

I also invest a day with a tourist guide who takes me to historical sites from the Spanish era, an ancient Catholic cathedral, Bohol's famous chocolate hills where vegetation turns brown and assumes the illusion of candy kisses, huge pettable anacondas, and tiny tarsiers, the world's smallest mammal.

For one week, I'm a tourist … and it feels good .

From the ambience of Bohol, I learn this about travel. Slow down. Be patient and flexible. Convert a long itinerary into short steps.

It is possible to fly non-stop from Delhi to Chicago; I did that last year, 15 hours in the same seat. No thank you. This year, I return to Michigan via a week in The Philippines and a week on Kauai. Fourteen days of beaches, water, and good food. No jet lag. What more can I say?

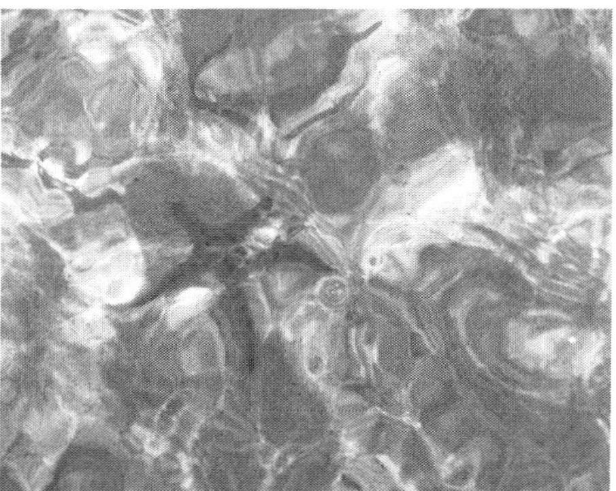

Below: This respite in paradise is capped off by four blind musicians singing "Unchained Melody" in the crowded Bohol Airport.

Travel … My Way

While, technically, I can get there from here, I sure don't like the itinerary. "Here" is Hawaii where, for 12 days, I'll work with a client on a book project. "There" is India where I'll help another client craft a manuscript about educating slum-dwelling children in Kolkata (Calcutta).

Every American-based airline will either zigzag me to Los Angeles and Amsterdam or all the way back to New Jersey for a non-stop from Newark. Total travel time: 48 hours—and expensive. Asia-based airlines offer a 42-hour itinerary with layovers in Shanghai, Tokyo, and Bangkok. While the East is on my bucket list, this isn't the way I want to visit those countries.

What to do? Hawaii is halfway across the Pacific, halfway between the U.S. mainland and the Indian subcontinent. There must be a decent route.

There is—with multiple airlines.

So, in July 2011, Delta takes me from Washington, D.C., where I heard the Dalai Lama, to Kauai then back to Detroit in February 2012; that's one liberally defined round trip. Hawaiian Air is my carrier between Kauai and Manila, outbound in July and homebound in January. And Philippine Air completes the middle segment from Manila to Delhi in August and back in January.

This patchwork flight plan presents opportunity. Not wanting to create tight connections, I schedule three days in The Philippines outbound, a week there homebound, and another week on Kauai homebound.

I also avoid hotels. While working in Kauai, I stay with my client. In Manila the first time, I stay in a compound operated by an NGO, thanks to a tip from Quaker friends in Kalamazoo. I also discover that three days in that city is enough, so at the recommendation of the NGO manager, I book a bonus round trip to the remote resort islands of Bohol and Panglao. On Kauai, again, I stay with neighbors of my client. And it's all good.

My client on Kauai is Toby Christensen, the Healing Drummer, who uses the djembe for sound therapy. Our work sessions include him standing over me, supine on the floor, creating rhythms with the massive drum inches above my chest. Oh, the things I do for research.

When not working, we walk water-lapped beaches, hike volcanic mountains, and sail on Hanalei Bay, home of Puff the Magic Dragon and Little Jackie Paper.

In India, I travel the dangerous Leh-Manali Highway to Leh (elev. 12,500 feet) looking for three women merchants I conversed with a year earlier, in July 2010. Exactly one week after my departure then, a killer flood, caused by a deluge, roared down the mountains and wiped out Leh's commercial market. I'm returning now to see if my friends are okay. They are. The rushing water passed them by with a margin of less than one kilometer.

I stay in a guesthouse on the village fringe. The view is of a stream, a wheat field, trees, and a ring of towering peaks. Guests dine outdoors, eating what the cook prepares with ingredients grown organically on the property. I fortuitously meet and accompany people from the NGOs Architects Without Borders and SEEDS India as they work to rebuild Ladakhi homes.

In Dharamsala, I attend three days of teaching by the Dalai Lama. I stay in a mountain guesthouse with black mold on the interior walls. While aesthetically attractive, I have no desire to sleep between the sheets, so I crawl into my sleeping bag, atop the covers—until moving into a Tibetan monastery. There, I sleep in a monk's cell, on a cot, next to a pane-less window while rock 'n' roll blasts from a nearby disco. I also spend hours laughing with my host monk, Gompo, age 22 or 24 (he doesn't have a birth certificate), and other monks to whom I teach English in the evenings. (Gompo is shown playing ping pong on page 49)

My client in Kolkata is Rosalie Giffoniello. For the past 11 years, she has lived and worked there to educate slum-dwelling children. The Indian government has decreed that every child is to receive an education, but that stipulation also requires uniforms, shoes, and books. Many families can't afford these, so slum children don't go to school. Rosalie, co-founder of Empower The Children, and others

like her have created "non-formal schools" to provide education without formalities—or books, which wouldn't survive incessant heat, humidity, dirt, and vermin.

Rosalie's flat, where I stay, is in a slum. Granted, it's a nice slum made of concrete as opposed to wood scraps and corrugated steel. But, it's still a slum—a *bhasti*—with unplanned architecture and neighbors who don't have legal rights to their residences.

The *basti* is beautiful in its simplicity and what we in the West would consider an old-time flavor. It's an urban village where adults and older siblings raise everyone's children. Their games are simple—hopscotch, tag, tops, caroms, kite flying (amazingly among buildings). Their toys don't require batteries, and their voices are rich with laughter and imaginative chatter.

Most of the residents are Muslim. The "call to prayer" is broadcast through megaphones, starting at 4:45 am. The imam's voice is melodic baritone; not understanding his words, I lie in bed and meditate my own prayers.

The laundry *dobie* and his family are Hindu. The tailor from whom I order shirts and *kurtas* is Sikh, as is the owner of a favorite eatery. The lady who cleans Rosalie's flat is Catholic, and she takes me to Mass in three different churches. Rosalie was raised Jewish but has adopted Buddhism. So, we have religious diversity right there within the flat.

I'm welcome in this *basti*. People invite me into their homes—single rooms about 15 by 15 for a family of ten. I enter dormitories, which are smaller yet, where a dozen men sleep on thin pieces of carpet or cardboard. Teens ask me to play caroms. I witness holy gatherings in the narrow streets and the slaughter of cattle, goats, and a camel for Eid al-Adha, the Islamic "Festival of Sacrifice," literally right outside my window.

The women, dressed in their beautiful, colorful *saris* are usually smiling. The children greet me with "Hello, Uncle," a carryover from the days of the British raj. The men, who gather within feet of my window each night to discuss religion, politics, or neighborhood affairs, readily switch to English when I join their discussion.

I attend a wedding anniversary party, a two-night affair on the roof of the building where we live, and weddings, which are five-day events. One man, whose daughter is one of the brides, grips my shoulders in his two hands, looks me strongly in the eyes, and insists, "You *must* come. You *must.*"

I live *among* these people—as Rosalie has for a decade—but I don't live *like* they do. I have my own bedroom, our private bathroom albeit with an Eastern-style squat toilet, a living room where we craft our book, a dining table, a water filter, a kitchen sans stove and oven.

Often, I wonder: Could I *truly live* as these people do?

If I were wealthy, I would have a flat and pay monthly rent of 11,000 rupees ($220). The landlord's two brothers and their families live in this building; they have nice furniture, large-screen televisions, ceiling fans, glass in the windows, a live-in maid.

But if my occupation were that of the fruit vendor who sells bananas for four rupees (six cents) or the cobbler whose "shop" is a blanket on the sidewalk, my intestinal system would have to learn how to drink unfiltered water from the community pump. My taste buds would have to like food laced with chilies. I would have to tolerate bathing and toileting in a wall-less area in the commons. I would wear flip-flops.

My residence would be a small room, shared with several others. Our door would be a curtain. We would have more spiders and lizards than the few who populate Rosalie's flat, and more mosquitoes and risk of malaria. I wouldn't have a computer and satellite Internet connection. I couldn't afford tickets to the Kolkata Film Festival.

I would also be living among poor people who exude sweet calmness, playfulness, happiness, joy. I would learn from them.

As it is, I fall asleep to their chatter, wake to their prayer, look out my window and see laundry strung in braided clotheslines or across a barbed wire fence, chat with men who cook *biryani*, win at caroms, and participate in religious festivals with a Muslim, Hindu, Sikh, or Jain friend at my side. That's travel … in my book.

Detroit Tigers Spring Training

A Fantastic Place A Fantastic Time

In February 2014, *Encore* correspondent Robert Weir attained a media pass to the Detroit Tigers spring training camp in Lakeland, Florida. With access to the field, the clubhouse, and the press box, he enjoyed a one-week close-up view into major league baseball. The following is his report—from a fan's perspective—along with some insight from former stars about how the game has changed during recent decades.

Photo courtesy Detroit Tigers

Come springtime, hope springs eternal in the world of baseball. And if you're a fan of the Tigers, Joker Marchant Stadium is the place to be. The weather is warm, the ballpark is cozy, the players are accessible for photos and autographs, and vendors offer fresh strawberry shortcake in addition to traditional hot dogs and brats.

On the field, the air is tickled with the crack of the bat against the ball and the smack of the ball into a glove. The players, most of them taller and larger than the average male, stretch, run, hit, field, throw and, almost every day, play a game of America's Game.

The fans, some from Michigan and some from Florida, are here to witness this rite of spring known as "spring training."

Baseball's preseason is unique among professional sport. Footballers practice on their home fields. Basketballers do likewise on their home courts. Hockey clubs might tour ice rinks in their home states; the Red Wings, for example, hold practice sessions in Traverse City.

But baseballers congregate in Florida and Arizona seven weeks before the start of their regular season. In open-air stadiums landscaped with palm trees, fans, many of them escaping from cold weather in wintry climes, enjoy blue skies, green grass and the umpire's pronouncement to "Play ball!"

The atmosphere in Lakeland is laid back. Players, management and stadium personnel know the fans are there for more than the game—they're there for the *experience,* whether seated in the stands or lounging on the famous "berm," a land formation that rises several feet above the homerun fence in left field.

Ruth Broadhurst and her husband, George, of Delton, are among hundreds on the berm. "We put spring training on our bucket list several years ago," she says. Then, with the winter of 2013–14 being abnormally cold, they decided, "This is the year; we're going." Their family's devotion to the Tigers is multi-generational. "Ruth's dad lived on a dairy farm and listened to the Tigers while milking," says George. "He said the cows gave more milk when the Tigers were winning."

The subjects of warm Florida temperatures and fan-player connections span from the stands to the clubhouse to the executive offices.

"Spring training is about getting our work done, coming together as a team and having fun," says new manager Brad Ausmus. "For the fans, it means knowing that summer is around the corner. Here in Lakeland, it's easier for them to get a player's autograph or shake a hand than during the regular season."

Tigers general manager, Dave Dombrowski, confirms, "Spring training reflects the start of baseball and warm weather. It's a way for us to get ready for the season, to get molded as a team." Of the atmosphere in Lakeland, he states, "There's more fan interaction—the facility is made so the players can sign autographs when they come off the field. It's a fantastic place, a fantastic time."

Bringing the scores, stats and scoops to the fans is the domain of the media corps who represent major internet, newspaper, television, and radio entities such as Major

League Baseball (MLB.com), MLive, *Detroit News, Detroit Free Press, USA Today* and Associated Press. The press box and the clubhouse are their daily beat, interviewing players as they lounge by their lockers in various stages of dress. For a few others, such as a reporter from a the Dominican Republic, the privilege of being here is more unique and the duration shorter—maybe a week at the most.

Each day, both pre-game and post-game, Tigers media relations people usher the dozen or so reporters into the manager's office, a cozy space with a single desk. A few correspondents sit on a couch; most stand. Ausmus directs one of the media stalwarts to sit in his chair behind the desk while taking a less auspicious seat himself.

The questions are of the daily grind: Who's going to pitch today? How is so-and-so's health? How will baseball's new replay rules affect the game? Do you see the Tigers stealing more bases this year? Ausmus answers each one with sincerity and detachment, giving detail when appropriate, being noncommittal when necessary, providing the guys and gals present with sufficient material to write their stories.

Willie Horton and Al Kaline are among the famous old-time Tigers in and around Joker Marchant Stadium, both retained by management as special assistants to team owner Mike Ilitch.

Horton, the Tigers left fielder from 1963 to 1977, encourages players to be like family. The youngest of 21 children, he speaks of his brothers, sisters, and minister who instilled him with character. He relates his first year as a Tiger when he, as a black man, walked six miles to the old Tiger Stadium because he couldn't get a ride in a white taxi. During the Motor City race riots of 1967, he stood atop his car, wearing

Fan interaction with Tiger players at Joker Marchant Stadium is exemplified in the two photos of All-Stars Miguel Cabrera (top) and Justin Verlander (bottom) with fans by the Tiger dugout during a game. Left: Willie Horton, the Tigers left fielder from 1963 to 1977, relates to the author about his attempts to restore peace in Detroit during the riots of 1967 and his current work Motor City youths.

his Tigers uniform, attempting to restore peace. He recalls celebrities working to get housing for black players. "Other players couldn't understand why we couldn't stay together," he explains.

Now involved with youth, wellness, and humanitarian programs in Detroit, his Horton Foundation provides scholarships for financially deprived inner-city youths. He's one of only four people the State of Michigan has honored with a legislated day; Rosa Parks is another.

Of the fans, Horton says, "They're extended family. When I was hurt, they got me through the pain. When I played and the team went on the road, I stayed with fans, had dinner with them. People would see us in a store or barbershop and they would talk to us. It's harder for the players to do that today; they don't have that freedom." He pauses, then concludes with a sincere smile, "I have a good, warm feeling being in Lakeland. I walk around here and say, 'Thank you.'"

Al Kaline, the Tigers All-Star right fielder from 1953 to 1974—his entire career—is revered as "Mr. Tiger." His presence on the field during spring training, wearing his uniform with the number 6 on the back, is an inspiration to the current players who he encourages to "enjoy and respect the game … to be mentally strong during the highs and lows."

Kaline broke into the Tigers starting lineup at age 18, fresh out of high school, one of only a handful of players to never play in the minor leagues. An All-Star for 18 of his 22 seasons, he was the first Tiger to be paid $100,000. "I'm blessed to still be in the game I love so much," states Kaline, now 79 and a member of the National Baseball Hall of Fame. He says being around the young players and their new slang makes him feel young. Of the weather, he adds, "People in Kalamazoo would love to be here."

Up in the press box, radio announcer Jim Price, the Tigers catcher from 1967 to 1973, says, "Ah, Kalamazoo!" Then adds his signature line, "Nice place!" and, "I get a lot of nice

How Has Baseball Changed?
An interview with Charlie "Paw Paw" Maxwell

Charlie Maxwell hailed from Paw Paw—thus his nickname. He broke into the major leagues with the Boston Red Sox in 1950 and played for the Detroit Tigers from 1955 to 1962. He led American League outfielders in fielding percentage in 1957 and 1960, with, amazingly, only one error in each of those seasons. He finished among the league leaders in homeruns four times. Retired from baseball since 1964, Maxwell and his wife, Ann, still live in the area. They have four children and 14 grandchildren.

Encore: How has spring training and baseball changed?

Maxwell: For us, spring training was for getting in shape. We all had jobs then and we worked up until the day before we had to go to Florida. We took our families. My wife homeschooled.

My starting salary was $5,000. We had to find a home in Florida and that cost was out our pocket. We also had to maintain our home in Paw Paw. So the money didn't go far.

I did winery work in the winter. So I got home from the baseball season in October and blended wine or grape juice during the winter.

Spring training was six weeks. It took a week to get the soreness out. Another three weeks to get in shape. The last two weeks were a drag.

Every player had to make all the road trips and play every day. For an away game, we would leave at six in the morning and get back at nine at night. That included two or three hours on a chartered Greyhound bus on two-lane roads.

(Note: Today, salaries are in the millions, players work out year-round, and often the star players don't travel to away games.)

In those days, we didn't interact with the fans like they do today. There were no throwing balls in the stands. That came in the 1990s, after the strike, when baseball knew it had to get fans back.

I was friends with Ted Williams; we had lockers next to each other. He taught me how to play the wall [the famous Green Monster in left field at Fenway Park]. When we were ahead, Ted would tell the coach to put me in the game. I threw left-handed and used to pitch batting practice to Ted so he could hit with a southpaw on the mound.

1955 and 1956 were my best years with Detroit. They called me "Sunday Punch" because I hit a lot of homeruns on Sunday.

Thank you for the article you wrote. Appreciate the way you captured the relationship between the city of Lakeland, the Detroit Tigers organization, and its fans. —Dave Dombrowski, President, General Manager, and Chief Executive Officer mail from the great fans on that side of the state." Of Lakeland, Price says, "There's an aura here. The players are more accessible than during the season. That's the big difference that makes spring training special."

Tom Gage, the beat writer for the *Detroit News* since 1979, offers that Joker Marchant Stadium is "an excellent ballpark that's more inviting, with more concessions and more comfort, than it used to be."

Don Westbury, one of the security guards who keeps fans from wandering into the clubhouse, says he's been a Tigers fan for 60 years. "I got my first Al Kaline autograph in 1955 when I was 11," he says. He explains that Joker Marchant Stadium was a training facility for the Army Air Corps during World War II. It became a ballpark in the late 1950s, named after Lakeland's director of Parks and Recreation at the time. "Joker was a great person who loved to be with people; and he loved baseball and the Tigers," Westbury adds.

A big change for the Tigers came at the end of 2013 with the retirement of "The Old Skipper" Jim Leyland. Yet Leyland was retained as an advisor and consultant, especially to Ausmus, the new manager. Often the two men, 25 years apart in age, stood together on the field, sharing observations and wisdom. Ever professional, though, Leyland remained in the background, acknowledging the leadership of the new field general.

Brad Asmus, in his first year of managing, confers with Jim Leyland, who had been the Tigers manager in previous years.

Likewise, Leyland's interviews were few, but one day he did gather an audience of reporters during the opposing team's batting practice. The location was near the Tigers clubhouse, next to the field and about 250 feet from home plate. That area is protected from flying baseballs by a pair of nets: one vertical, 60 feet away from where the cadre stood, and the other horizontal, directly above—but the two don't meet. Sure enough, a foul ball found the gap and traced a perfect trajectory toward the back of Leyland's head.

The reporters facing the ball saw it coming but were too far away to protectively react. Fortunately, Aileen Villarreal, the Tigers director of Media Relations, who was standing at Leyland's left shoulder, caught a glimpse of the fast-dropping white orb and darted her hand, deflecting it at the last split second and saving Leyland from a painful conk on the noggin.

Inevitably, some baseball games are rained out. During one downpour, thousands of fans huddled in the concrete concourse under the seats above. They talked about their love of the game. Some spoke about why they were in Lakeland.

Johanna Kahny and Nicole Millering, students at Grand Valley State College, know shortstop Hernan Perez. "He lived with my grandma, a host family, when he was with the White Caps [the Tigers minor league affiliate in Grand Rapids]," said Nicole.

John Holmes of Kalamazoo says he likes spring training because "they change pitchers a lot more, so you get more variety. The excitement of it all makes it fun."

Lindsay and Ken Dood of Grand Rapids like that "at spring training, you get to see the players closer up than at Comerica Park. It's a lot more relaxed, so the players are more willing to talk to you and give autographs. This is our first time, and we're having a blast!"

But perhaps the best compliment to baseball's appeal over time comes from the perspectives of age and youth.

Boomer Mentzer of Kalamazoo, who is in his 60s, has been coming to spring training since he was a teenager. He's been to Florida to see the Tigers and Arizona to watch the Chicago Cubs. "Baseball is baseball and I love it. It's in my blood." Of a special experience, he adds, "Once, a lady I was with got a kiss from Lance Parrish, [Tigers catcher, 1977 to 1986, and now manager of the Seawolves, a Tigers farm club in Erie, Pennsylvania]."

And from Brennan Ansell, age 12, of Battle Creek, who was at the game with his father, Spencer, and grandparents Judy and Bill Ansell, comes the charm of youth. "I grew up watching Tiger baseball. I would like to meet Justin Verlander and ask him how he stays accurate with this pitching."

From my perspective as a longtime fan who claims Kaline as a boyhood hero? Well, I simply smile and await, once again, that welcome cry: "Play ball!"

John McConnell

The Man Who Planted Earth Day's Grass Roots

People in various parts of the planet celebrate Earth Day on *two different dates*. Both Earth Days are annual events. Both originated in the United States in 1970. One started with a goal of increasing environmental awareness in the United States. The other started with a goal of increasing global peace and cooperation as well as Earth appreciation. One Earth Day takes place on April 22. The other occurs a month earlier on the spring equinox.

This is the story of those two Earth Days and the founder of the *original* Earth Day, global visionary John McConnell. One of my grandest adventures was learning about John then interviewing him and writing his story. My greatest piece of journalism is his biography, *Peace, Justice, Care of Earth,* which I researched and crafted in 2004 through 2006.

* * * * *

Earth Day 1970 was a hallmark event in the chronicles of the environmental movement, and it stemmed from a pressing need.

Starting five centuries earlier, European settlers arrived in and pressed across North America. Initially, they traveled west on foot and with horse- or oxen-drawn wagons. Then, they strung telegraph lines, laid railroad tracks and, finally, poured ribbons of highways to communicate and commute both west and east.

By the 1960s, the land and waterways from sea to shining sea were more than tainted by humanity who seemed to eschew preservation because—they believed—more virgin resources could always be found over the next hill or a little farther upstream.

But it was not so. In the extreme, Lake Erie, part of the world's greatest supply of fresh surface water, was declared dead when the Cuyahoga River, near Cleveland, Ohio, caught fire, on June 22, 1969. Ignitable pollutants floating on the surface were sparked into flame by a passing train, and flames 50 feet high drifted with the current and destroyed railroad bridges under which the burning slick passed.

On the social and political front, the nation was sorrowed and angered by the assassination of Dr. Martin Luther King, Jr., in April 1968 and the multitude of deaths, measured in hundreds of thousands, caused by the Vietnam War throughout the decade. Many believed that entry into the 1970s warranted a new paradigm.

Amidst these dramas, the environmental movement came of age on Earth Day 1970, and people of Kalamazoo were involved. Loy Norrix High School administrators and teachers bicycled to work. Students from South Westnedge Elementary planted twenty-two yews on school property. Millwood Junior High pupils created skits and watched environmental movies. Boy Scouts and Girl Scouts picked up litter.

Kalamazoo College students cleaned debris from nearby Arcadia Creek, held a symposium and planted trees on campus. To capacity crowds at Stetson Chapel, Michigan Governor William G. Milliken spoke against pollution and Kalamazoo Nature Center Director H. Lewis Batts talked about mankind's role in ecology.

Nazareth College, which held graduation services in the third week of April, conducted an elaborate pollution awareness campaign in mid-March. Having sent invitations to school districts throughout Kalamazoo County and surrounding areas, Nazareth was rewarded with tremendous turnout by both young people and adults who were then transported on public school buses to industrial pollution sites in Kalamazoo and Portage. Some of those sites later became the recipients of federal funds for pollution cleanup.

Western Michigan University, which also graduated its Class of 1970 in April, celebrated the event on Saturday, March 14. Students created a morbid display of "earth reality if pollution continues," distributed flyers about phosphate-laden detergents to shoppers at major grocery stores, and showed a movie, *Our Poisoned World.*

Western's President James W. Miller, Michigan Senator

Phillip Hart, Dr. Batts, and representatives from Allied Paper, General Motors and The Upjohn Company participated in a panel discussion in the Student Center where slides revealed local pollution sites; Senator Sander Levin

WMU's student newspaper, *Western Herald*, provided extension coverage of campus and national Earth Day events, including a special eight-page supplement that included a photo spread with the headline "An Arrogant Generation Polluting Beyond Belief."

Quite accurately, both on the local and national scene, the *Kalamazoo Gazette* reported in a front-page article, "Students—from kindergarten to graduate school—were putting the polluters and litterbugs of the word on notice that they are concerned about the survival of the world they live in."

That concern—a paradigm shift—resulted in U.S. legislation that included the Clean Air Act (amended 1970), Clean Water Act (1972), Safe Drinking Water Act (1974), Resource Conservation and Recovery Act (1976), and Toxic Substances Control Act (1976).

The U.S. and Canada signed (1972), then renewed (1978), the Great Lakes Water Quality Agreement to restore and maintain the chemical, physical, and biological integrity of the Great Lakes Basin ecosystem.

The Earth Day events described above occurred in most parts of the nation on Wednesday, April 22, 1970.

The idea was conceived by Wisconsin Senator Gaylord Nelson, who, for most the 1960s, had tried in vain to bring environmental issues to the political forefront. An environmental awareness tour that included President John F. Kennedy and several senators in the Fall of 1963 did not produce the desired results.

But on that Wednesday in 1970, more than 20 million people spoke out against pollution, and credit for the event lies with Nelson's persistence and his cadre of political staffers and student volunteers as well as their ability to generate massive public awareness.

But April 22, 1970, was not the *first* Earth Day. Nor was April 22, at first, called "Earth Day."

The original Earth Day occurred on a smaller scale, primarily in California, on the spring equinox, March 21, 1970. It spread to the United Nations, New York City's Central Park, and other venues in 1971. It has, since, become known worldwide as "International Earth Day" or "Equinox Earth Day" mostly to avoid confusion with *the other* Earth Day.

This Equinox Earth Day was the idea of Earth evangelist and visionary John McConnell, who devoted his life to the three-part tenet of "peace, justice and the care of Earth."

Seeing decades earlier the same pollution that others finally saw in the 1960s, John McConnell looked deeper for the root cause. He realized that environmental degradation did not originate with pollution but with a collective mindset that permitted pollution. But unlike Senator Nelson, McConnell possessed neither a political forum nor a public relations infrastructure to help deliver his message.

Also, unlike Nelson, McConnell's message was multi-faceted. Speaking generally alone, McConnell stressed that the *care of Earth* is, first, dependent upon *peace*, which John defined not as "the end of war—that's an armistice," but "honest agreement based on understanding and harmony and cooperation." *Peace*, in turn, he said is dependent upon *justice*, which is not a judicial "eye for an eye and a tooth for a tooth," but "an equal sharing of nature's bounty, a right of all people for planetary inheritance."

He often stated, "Environmental efforts by themselves will leave us in ruins unless we promote peace and unless we have economic justice."

With evangelistic audacity, John took his message to receptive audiences as well as to those less willing to listen. To an Iranian oil sheikh, he said, "You should pay a royalty to the owners of the oil you take, and that's all the people of Earth."

Obviously oil barons, foreign and domestic, have not followed that admonition. However, Walter J. Hickel, former Governor of Alaska, did. After meeting with John McConnell, Hickel established the program through which all citizens of that state receive a share of proceeds from oil extracted under Alaskan soil.

Regardless of the natural resource, John professed that a handful of people should not profit, at the expense of the majority, from resources they did not create. Such resources—"gifts from God for all humankind"—are not only oil but gold, silver, platinum, virgin timber, water "and other common properties that nobody makes."

Similarly, John intended Earth Day to be a "global holiday." For months in 1969, he considered various dates, seeking the *one* to which all people of the planet could relate.

Then while visiting his mother in Oakland, California, he happened upon a book about Stonehenge, the ancient sarsen configuration in southern England created by Druids as a megalithic celestial calendar. He told his wife, Anna, that Earth Day should be on the spring equinox, "nature's event." At that moment, the McConnells felt a slight tremor, a minor earthquake, an indication in their minds that Earth—or God—was confirming his inspiration.

Two months later, in November 1969, John announced his idea at a meeting of United Nations Educational, Scientific and Cultural Organization (UNESCO) in San Francisco. This major international event was attended by over 400 dignitaries, scientists, educators, business people, politicians, representatives of labor unions, the media, various environmental and civic associations and private citizens.

Immediately after his speech, two young men introduced themselves as aides to Senator Nelson and invited him to join their campaign, which they said would be an "Environmental Teach-In," patterned after "teach-ins" that had become popular on college campuses as a mechanism to protest the Vietnam War.

John listened to the invitation. He recognized the date they were proposing. April 22 was also Arbor Day, founded in Nebraska in 1872 by J. Sterling Morton.

But his young suitors didn't mention that historical connection. Instead, they posed pragmatic reasons for having selected April 22: It was mid-week, midway between spring break and final exams on most campuses, and the weather would likely be favorable in northern climates. Good reasons, from a public relations perspective, but inherently incongruous with John's objectives of global peace, social justice, and Earth care. "Absolutely not," he replied. "The global history and symbolism of having Earth Day on the equinox is too great."

On February 11, 1970, San Francisco Mayor Joseph Alioto signed the first official Earth Day proclamation, declaring "March 21st (Vernal Equinox) to be designated EARTH DAY—a special day to remember Earth's tender seedlings of life and people; a day for planting trees and flowers; a day for cleaning streams and wooded glens." Berkeley mayor Wallace Johnson signed a similar proclamation, as did mayors and city councils throughout various parts of California.

John then worked with students at the University of California in Davis who responded with week-long campus activities, called "Whole Earth Week, An Aquarian Festival of Life," that included a demonstration of an energy-efficient geodesic dome, custom posters by artist Peter Max, meditations by Swami Shatidananda, and participation by priests, pastors, and rabbis. John's friends and colleagues in New York and Washington, D.C. also promoted Earth Day events on the east coast.

Then, on January 18, 1970, thunder struck. John received a phone call from his attorney in the nation's capitol. The attorney stated, "I thought Earth Day was going to be on the spring equinox." John replied, "It is." To which the attorney returned, "Well, *The Washington Post* and *The New York Times* just ran full-page ads announcing Earth Day on April 22."

Years later, correspondence from Senator Nelson to a friend of John McConnell's stated that the senator didn't know where the name of Earth Day originated, possibly "a friend in public relations [or] a New York advertising executive." The letter also stated that "the press increasingly referred to it as Earth Day."

In other communications from an associate of Senator Nelson to John McConnell, the associate told John he suggested the name Earth Day because he had seen "an item in the papers about some kids in California who were planning an Earth Day."

John was incensed. "Christmas wouldn't be the same if we celebrated it all year long. The same with your birthday." Those words prophesized confusion about the two Earth Days that would follow for many years.

In spite of the words "Earth Day" in those major newspaper ads, Senator Nelson continued to use the term "National Environmental Teach-In" in his public dialogue in 1970, and he established a nonprofit organization called "The Environmental Teach-In, Inc."

Speaking at the University of Michigan in April 1970, he titled his address "Ann Arbor Teach-In," and his schedule for the week of April 20-24 was headlined "Teach-In Tour." But in 1971, Senator Nelson began to promote an "Earth Week" for mid- to late-April.

In the meantime, John McConnell took his idea for the spring equinox Earth Day to the United Nations, with which he had a five-year professional association. At his request, mayors in New York, Baltimore, and other eastern cities declared the spring equinox to be Earth Day in 1971 and subsequent years.

In 1972, he co-produced a 12-hour environmental special on WOR-TV in New York that was hosted by Hugh Downs and featured nationally known social and environmental experts.

Both Earth Days received Congressional support. In 1971, the U.S. House of Representatives passed a resolution designating "March 21, the vernal equinox, of each year as 'Earth Day.'" Then, in 1973, the U.S. Senate passed a resolution making April 9-15 Earth Week.

The situation oscillated in similar fashion in the White House where President Richard Nixon proclaimed April 17-23, 1972, as Earth Week; President Gerald Ford signed a national proclamation for the equinox Earth Day in 1975; and President Jimmy Carter did the same for April 22 in 1980.

Various state governors signed proclamations for one day or the other in the early 1970s. Governor Arch A. Moore, Jr., of West Virginia, for example, proclaimed April 9-15, 1973, to be Earth Week, in accordance with the U.S. Senate resolution, but wrote to his fellow governors his desire that they observe "the first day of spring as Earth Day" the following year.

Perhaps the confusion was best

summarized in a letter from Governor Milliken to Governor Linwood Holton of Virginia in 1973 in which the Michigan head of state exclaimed "the need for coordination and consistency in our observations of Earth Day. Just this year, for example, I was asked to declare three different dates as Earth Day or Earth Week by differing organizations."

Eventually, the political momentum of Senator Nelson's forces prevailed in the United States while the Equinox Earth Day continued in favor with the United Nations where it gained immediate attention in countries around the world.

At the UN in 1971, Secretary-General U Thant rang the Peace Bell, located in a garden at the institution's international headquarters New York, at 2:00 pm on Sunday, 21 March—the vernal equinox.

Secretary-General Kurt Waldheim rang the Peace Bell for the Earth Day celebration in 1972. Waldheim's chief de cabinet, C. V. Narasimhan, rang it on Tuesday, 20 March, 1973, at precisely 1:13 pm. He, thus, began a tradition that has continued every year since; that is, ringing the Peace Bell at the exact moment of equipoise in New York City, even if it occurs in the middle of the night.

Other UN Peace Bell ringers have included anthropologist Margaret Mead; astronaut Dr. Edward Gibson; Canadian parliamentarian Paul McRae; representatives to the UN from the U.S., USSR and the Muslim World League; former Iran hostage Joseph Ciccipio; a child from Israel and a child from Palestine; Anna McConnell and friend Hans Janitschek; Shimon Peres, foreign minister of Israel; New York mayor Rudolph Giuliani; Frank O. Braynard, who organized the bicentennial tall ships festival in New York Harbor in 1976; and folk singer Pete Seeger.

Interestingly enough, John McConnell, the man who started Earth Day, waited 34 years—until two days prior to his 89th birthday in 2004—for the honor of ringing the Peace Bell. When he did, the crowd was sparse and the event drew no media attention, probably because of the hour—1:49 a.m. on Saturday, March 20. But, in some ways, that moment in the after-midnight hours of a chill New York morning speaks volumes about John McConnell—a man of devout courage and inadequate acclaim.

Reflecting on his life, John admits failure because of "the contradictions that you find in Earth Day." By this, he references, not only the confusion between two Earth Days, but a much larger contradiction. Exactly one year earlier, on March 20, 2003, the day of the year that John McConnell hoped would symbolize global peace and unity, his country, the United States of America, attacked Iraq. With that war still raging a year later, John intoned in his passionate, ever-modulating centurion voice, "We've got to kill our terrible addiction to war. We ought to make friends—and not skeletons—of our enemies."

In calmer reverie, John also recalls the words of his friend and associate Margaret Mead, with whom he founded the Earth Society Foundation in 1976. When honored with the privilege of ringing the Peace Bell in 1977, Mead spoke an ultimate tribute to the spirit of John McConnell's Equinox Earth Day.

"Earth Day," the famous anthropologist said, "is to be the first completely international and universal holiday that the world has ever known. Every other holiday was tied to one place, or some political or special event. This Day is tied to Earth itself, and to the place of Earth in the whole solar system. At this moment, when I climb the steps and ring the Peace Bell, it will be the Equinox in every part of the world, and we can all celebrate it at once on behalf of every part of the world."

That theme of "nature's global holiday for all of Earth's citizens" is the goal that John McConnell, now in his 90th year, still hopes to see in his lifetime.

(Author's Note: John McConnell passed from this life on October 20, 2012. His remains are buried in Mountain Grove Cemetery in Bridgeport, Connecticut. He is survived by Anna, his daughter Christa, and her family.)

John McConnell is also the creator of the Earth Flag, "The Flag for All People" and the only flag not associated with nationalism, consumerism, or competition. Top photo: John and Anna hold one of the original Earth Flags, a two-color silkscreen with blue and white to represent the globally shared substances of water and air (clouds). Lower photo: Anna and John with one of the current Earth Flags that is adorned with a full-color photograph of Earth that was taken by astronauts on the Apollo 17 moon mission on December 7, 1972. Once trademarked by John and his successors, the Earth Flag is now in the public domain.

Writing John McConnell's Biography

This full-color, five-foot by twelve-foot mural panel was created as a tribute to John and Anna McConnell by muralists Joanne Tawfilis and Cady Macasa as part of the Art Miles Mural project in Denver; it was unveiled in April 2005.

I learned of John McConnell in early 2001 when my church asked me to speak about the environment on the Sunday before Earth Day (April 22). While gathering information, I discovered John McConnell's web site.

Impressed with the depth, richness and spirit of John's essays, I quoted him and sent a courtesy e-mail to him, saying that I was doing so. Three days later, he telephoned me and asked if I would write his biography.

At the time, I was not able to begin the project, but did so in earnest in 2004 when I visited John and Anna at their home in Denver—first for three days, then later for six weeks. I also heard John speak and ring the Peace Bell at the 2004 Earth Day ceremony at the United Nations.

In 2005, I began to research the thousands of paper documents—essays, speeches, correspondence, news releases, newspaper clippings, and financial records—that John and Anna donated to the Peace Collection at Swarthmore College, a Quaker institution near Philadelphia.

I learned that writing a biography involves jigsaw puzzling and forensics. Through conversation with John and Anna, I constructed the frame, or outer edge, of the puzzle of his life. At Swarthmore, the paper documents, especially letters, filled in the inner, deeper picture.

For example, John and Anna told me of their two children and that John Paul, the elder, had Downs Syndrome and died as an infant while Anna was pregnant with Christa. They told me of John's major accomplishments, including the Earth Flag and Earth Day. What they told me was like saying that the jigsaw puzzle picture has two trees, two children, and a storm cloud.

The forensics study at Swarthmore has revealed that, in the two years between June 1968 and May 1970, the couple experienced the birth of their son in Brooklyn, a move to Virginia where the child received specialized treatment for daily convulsions, John's development and introduction of the Earth Flag to coincide with Neil Armstrong's first step on the moon, extended visits to John's mother in California and to Anna's mother in Connecticut, the death of their son and the birth of their daughter, John's announcement regarding Earth Day at a United Nations conference in San Francisco, the first Earth Day with all of its organization and promotion, and fulfillment of hundreds of Earth Flag orders for which Anna kept *handwritten* records and *typed* acknowledgements and thank you notes.

With this detail, I was able to see the daily adventure and commitment of their lives in the same way that a puzzler finds pieces that give shadow and highlight to wind-bent trees, tempest rain, brilliant lightning bolts, and the expressions of concern on the children's faces.

Fortunately, I like puzzles and would have enjoyed a career in forensics. So this project was fun—and worthwhile, for I also believe in John and Anna's mission of "peace, justice and the care of Earth." I am proud to be their biographer.

A Kalamazoo Perspective on the United Nations

By Robert M. Weir

Writer Robert Weir stands in the United Nations General Assembly hall prior to the start of the 58th annual conference on nongovernmental organizations. Weir attended the UN event as a correspondent for Encore Publishing Group. Photo composite by *Encore Magazine*.

The Pursuit of Peace

One year ago, *Encore* published an article I wrote about visionary John McConnell, the man who started the original Earth Day, created the Earth Flag, and founded a United Nations non-governmental organization (NGO). At that time, I was enmeshed with writing John McConnell's biography and learning about his life-long dedication to "peace, justice, and the care of Earth."

To better understand the venue in which he moved, I visited the UN on several occasions over the last two years. There, I observed Earth Day celebrations, NGO conferences, and a rare World Summit that featured the world's heads of state. I even took the standard UN visitor's tour. This article is an account of that adventure.

* * * * *

The Earth Day ceremony at the UN is hosted by the Earth Society Foundation, the NGO that John McConnell created. The first ceremony occurred in 1971; Secretary-General U Thant rang the Peace Bell, which resides in an oriental garden next to the UN Secretariat Building in New York City.

In that first year and again in 1972, when Secretary-General Kurt Waldheim rang the Peace Bell, the ceremony occurred at 2:00 p.m. Eastern Time. However, since then, the ceremony has surrounded the moment of equipoise, as determined by the tilt of Planet Earth.

In 2004, the first time I visited the UN, John McConnell rang the Peace Bell at 1:39 a.m. It was cold in New York that night, and the few people who attended were bundled in winter coats and scarves. Yet, the mood was festive because, even though John had initiated the Earth Day ceremony 33 years prior, it was the first time he, at age 88, had performed the ceremony's principal function.

The following year, in 2005, Aye Aye Thant, daughter of U Thant and president of the U Thant Institute, rang the Peace Bell along with three UN ambassadors. That ceremony occurred at 7:33 a.m. I was privileged to meet Ms. Thant and create an acquaintance through which she provided information for John's biography.

Afterward, many attendees adjourned to a nearby building for a breakfast reception. There, standing on a dais with an Earth Flag draped on the wall behind me, I told that international audience of my project. It was a thrilling step in the journey of crafting John's life into text.

I also reflected on the Peace Bell, itself, and the honor bestowed upon those privileged to ring it.

The Peace Bell is a unique symbol. Standing a little over three feet tall, two feet wide and weighing 256 pounds, it was cast on United Nations Day, 24 October 1952, by Japan even though that Pacific island nation had not yet gained admission to the world body.

The metal in the bell consists of coins, collected by children from delegates of sixty countries at a UN conference in Paris, France, in 1951. Inscribed inside the bell, in the Japanese language, are the words: "Long live absolute peace."

It was installed at the UN on 8 June 1954, but until the Earth Day ceremony in 1971, was rung only twice: at the time of installation, and on 4 October 1966 to commemorate the first anniversary of an historic visit to the UN by Pope Paul VI. John McConnell was instrumental in making the Peace Bell part of that event.

On 8 June 2004, I observed a ceremony to mark the 50th anniversary of the Peace Bell's installation. The event was in the middle of the afternoon on a glorious sunny day. New York traffic bustled by on First Avenue as the banner of each nation, aligned in alphabetical order according to the English language, thrummed atop flag poles near the UN visitors entrance. Secretary-General Kofi Annan delivered brief remarks, then rang the bell.

My next trip to the UN occurred in late May 2005. I had finished reading thousands of John McConnell's papers that he and his wife, Anna, donated to the Swarthmore College Peace Collection archives near Philadelphia, Pennsylvania, and I wanted to treat myself to a casual trip to New York.

At a UN forum on water, I heard Dr. Masaru Emoto speak in his native Japanese language, through a translator, about the impact of words on water—and consequently on human health. Dr. Emoto spoke about the concepts in his best-selling book *The True Power or Water: Healing and Discovering Ourselves.*

He pointed out that the adult human body is 70 percent water; a newborn's body is 90 percent water. "If the water content in our body drops only a little, that's dehydration, and we can die," Dr. Emoto declared.

Then, Dr. Emoto projected photographs of ice crystals taken via a microscope in his laboratory. Some were exquisite and others were downright ugly. Dr. Emoto stated that the clear, beautiful crystals formed from water that had been stored in bottles labeled with words like "love," "peace" and "thank you." In contrast, the discolored and malformed crystals came from water stored in bottles labeled "hate," "war" and "you fool."

Dr. Emoto emphasized the water in both sets originated from the same source—purified spring water. His presentation revealed the bottles had been labeled in various languages—Japanese, English, French and others—with comparable results.

Dr. Emoto hypothesized the water wasn't so much affected by static words on the label as it was by active thoughts of the person handling the water; that is, a person reading "love" or "hate" conveyed vibrational thought energy to the water.

To exemplify that concept, he utilized two tuning forks, both created to vibrate at Middle C. As he struck one with a mallet, both emitted sound—the second set in motion by invisible energy vibrations from the first.

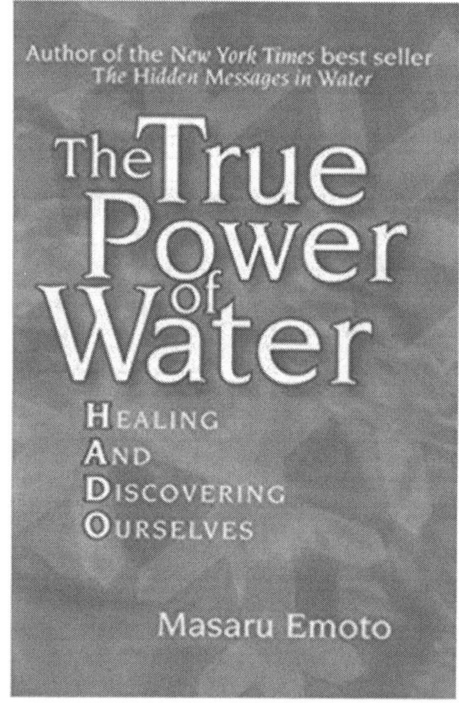

As Dr. Emoto told of prayer circles he has convened around polluted lakes, I considered a phrase from my youth about "bad vibes" and "good vibes," the concept that "every thought is a prayer," and John McConnell's oft-repeated phrase, "Oh, the faith that works by love will move mountains when we pray."

Then, in contrast, I reflected on adults who blaspheme children, spouses who exchange cruelties, and violence in entertainment, and I cringed at the evil power of angry, hateful words and images that maladjust our young, our families, our society.

At that moment, I acquired greater appreciation for the United Nations. Clearly, this forum, which was sponsored by NGOs involved with human values, spirituality, and religious initiatives, embodied a part of the world organ not reported by mainstream media. Yet, it was an integral element within the UN mission: "to practice tolerance and live together in peace with one another as good neighbours."

My greatest immersion into the UN occurred in September 2005 when I attended two major events: an annual conference of non-governmental organizations and the World Summit.

From a tour guide, I learned the United Nations was founded in 1945 in San Francisco when China, France, Russia, the United Kingdom, and the United States came together at the end of World War II to establish a global governmental organization to prevent future wars.

At that time, the UN's initial roll included 51 Member States. Today, the United Nations has its primary headquarters in the 39-story Secretariat Building along New York City's East River, with primary satellite offices in Geneva, Switzerland, and Vienna, Austria, plus secondary facilities in several other cities.

In 60 years, the borders of the geopolitical world have changed significantly, and the number of countries represented in the UN General Assembly has grown to 191—all but three in the world. However, the UN's primary power unit, the Security Council, is still comprised of the original five permanent countries plus ten non-permanent members.

But some people want to change the UN's structure to better represent the world's current conditions. Among them is Kofi Annan, the seventh person to serve as Secretary-General. On 21 March 2005, he released a report about United Nations reform, titled *In Larger Freedom*, in which he wrote, in order to promote human rights, democracy and development, "We must reshape the Organization in ways not previously imagined and with a boldness and speed not previously known."

The message of United Nations reform is also being spoken by over 4,000 non-governmental organizations. NGOs, collectively known as "civil society," are non-profit, volunteer citizens' groups, created on a local, national, or international level to perform humanitarian functions and facilitate actions of public good. Some are organized around specific issues, such as children and disabled persons, crime prevention and drug control, education and hunger, religion and peace, trade and technology, and health and environment.

A few NGOs, for example, are AARP, Africa Action on AIDS, Asia Crime Prevention Foundation, Baptist World Alliance, Franciscans International, Global Environmental Action, Habitat for Humanity, Human Rights Watch, Humane Society, Muslim World League, The Nature Conservancy, The Population Council, Rotary International, The Salvation Army, and Women's International Network.

Each NGO affiliated with the UN must have been in existence for at least three years and show signs of sustained activity. And, while most are not allowed to speak at UN formal sessions, they provide information to ambassadors and monitor actions by Members States.

To that end, a record 1,800 representatives of 700 NGOs from 86 countries gathered at the UN for their 58th annual conference on 7 to 9 September 2005. Fifteen percent of the attendees traveled from developing countries.

The title of the conference, "Our Challenge: Voices for Peace, Partnerships and Renewal," embodied their goal. Delegates and speakers expressed two concerns: the lack of cooperation among a few Member States to implement change within the UN, if not a move by some ambassadors to actually weaken the UN; and the lack of progress on eight initiatives known as the Millennium Development Goals (MDGs) that the Member States, in 2000, pledged to achieve by 2015.

In general, the MDGs will reduce or eradicate poverty, hunger, child mortality, and infectious diseases such as malaria and HIV/AIDS. The MDGs will also improve primary education, gender equality, maternal health, the environment, and the fate of developing countries. More specifically, MDG language shows the dire straits of too many of the world's people. Goal #1, for example, intends to "reduce by half the proportion of people living on less than a dollar a day."

Display boards in UN corridors dynamically portrayed the degree of disparity among the world's peoples:

- the percentage of babies delivered by health professionals is 99% in the United Kingdom and only 22% in Yemen;
- the death rate of children under age five is 0.3% in Sweden and 28.4% in Sierra Leone;
- life expectancy at birth is 82 years in Japan and 38 years in Zambia; and
- the average years of schooling is 11.6 in Canada compared to 2.4 in Nepal.

The display stated, "Halving extreme poverty by 2015 is doable but will not happen unless government and civil society act to close the ever-widening disparity between countries and within countries."

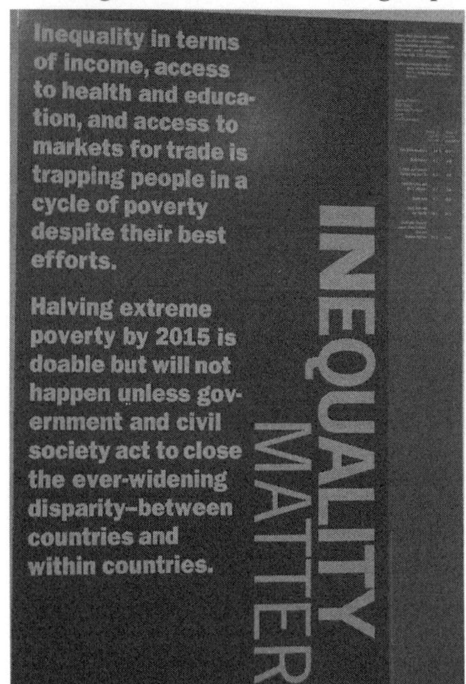

Death rate of children under five

Sweden 0.3%

Sierra Leone 28.4%

INEQU

This message of choice and action was most evident in a chart on the guided tour. An inverted triangle was divided into two portions. The larger top represented the amount of money spent by nations *annually* on military and weapons—$800 billion. The smaller bottom showed the amount of money—$212.5 billion—needed *once* to resolve world maladies as defined in the MDGs.

I couldn't help but think that too many world leaders are obsessed with ill-fated priorities, choosing to spend much more on death and destruction than on peace, prosperity, and human values.

In accord with that thought, the NGOs, in their plenary and seminar sessions, took a vocal stance, claiming that Member States, with few exceptions, have done little—or not enough—to meet the MDGs in the five years since they were agreed upon.

The NGOs proclaimed, "2015 is NOW!" They approved a resolution: "We … urge leaders at this crucial time in the world's need for human security, peace and development, [to] embrace the larger vision of the United Nations to benefit all the people of the world. We urge you to yield narrow interests and to work with each other for real change expressed in concrete, practical terms. Please do not squander this important opportunity."

Only five days later, on 14 September, the UN was populated by presidents, prime ministers, and potentates of almost every Member State. Security around the world headquarters was heightened accordingly.

In possession of my media badge as an *Encore* correspondent, I joined a throng of media personnel from around the world as we stood in a 300-foot line for three hours to pass through metal detectors tuned to maximum sensitivity. There, in line, I spoke with correspondents from Brazil, Argentina, and the United Kingdom.

Coming out the rear of the security tent, I found myself gazing upon the East River with an anchored U.S. Coast Guard vessel and patrolling New York City police boats. Dressed in dark suit and tie and carrying my backpack with laptop, I found the sun bright and the temperature hot for September. Yet, I lingered to gaze at the scene, while noting again the absence of traffic on First Avenue, which was cordoned off with police barricades and cars with flashing blue lights.

Passing the UN courtyard, I found unsettling irony in a bronze sculpture of a naked, muscled man with hammer raised to strike his sword and words carved into its stone base: "We shall beat our swords into plowshares." I wondered what was happening inside the Secretariat Building: conflict or cooperation?

The answer to that question came by watching speeches by world leaders on closed circuit monitors in the media room. Over the next three days, I observed neither open conflict nor full cooperation, rather diplomatic, yet adversarial, rhetoric.

Developed countries in North America and Europe, for the most part, advocated "free trade" that would allow further despoilment of natural resources. In contrast, developing countries, primarily in Asia, Africa, and South America, spoke of "fair trade" and "human rights" that would help poorer people gain parity with the rest of the world's population.

This lack of common view was most apparent in a session of the Security Council. In a 90-minute meeting full of formality and prepared statements—and, thus, devoid of discussion—the heads of state unanimously passed two resolutions: one on terrorism, and the other on conflict in Africa. But while the men and women there spoke in favor of deeper cooperation among Member States, they proposed dissimilar solutions.

U.S. President George W. Bush, England's Prime Minister Tony Blair, Denmark's Prime Minister Andres Fogh Rasmussen, and Gloria Macapagal Arroyo, President of The Philippines, for example, used fear-based words like "extremism" and "fanaticism" to state their belief that terrorism can only be defeated by killing terrorists.

In contrast, French Prime Minister Dominique de Villepin, President Lula da Silva of Brazil, Romanian President Traian Basescu, and Benin President Mathieu Kerekou conveyed their preference to focus on the causes of terrorism. Their speeches advocated "preventing terror from breeding in hotbeds of hopelessness," and taking "resolute action on everything that fuels terrorism."

The World Summit ended on 16 September with the General Assembly's approval of a compromise plan to reorganize the UN. While the decision was unanimous, statements after the vote revealed dissent, disappointment, and resigned acceptance that partial reform was better than no reform.

Top photo: United Nations Secretary-General Kofi Annan is poised to ring the Japanese Peace Bell in the Rose Garden on the UN grounds in New York City. Lower photo: The Secretary-General and his wife, Nane, mingle among dignitaries and citizens at the ceremony to mark the beginning of the UN's 60th annual session on 21 September 2005.

A week after the World Summit concluded, on 21 September, Secretary-General Kofi Annan rang the Peace Bell, marking the beginning of the 60th annual session of the General Assembly; it was also the International Day of Peace.

I was amazed at the absence of pomp and circumstance—the almost informality—of the event. As a correspondent, I had no greater privilege than any other attendee, yet, I obtained great, close-up photographs of Mr. Annan, his wife Nane, dignitaries and media celebrities. As the Secretary-General milled about the garden, he passed within arms reach of where I was standing.

Security? Well, yes, my laptop case and I had passed through metal detectors at the visitors entrance earlier, but still ... I was amazed to be this close to the Secretary-General of the United Nations.

Yet, my eyes were opened further two days later on Friday, 23 September, in Washington, D.C. I had gone to the U.S. capital to participate in the demonstration against the War in Iraq to be held on Saturday. With an extra day at my disposal, I attended an annual legislative conference, hosted by the Congressional Black Caucus, about Africa at which Kofi Annan was the keynote speaker.

I entered the Washington Convention Center along with hundreds of government personnel and members of the public. I walked into the conference room and sat in the third row. With Mr. Annan at the head table, he was no more than 20 feet away.

There was no security check here, neither at the convention center entrance nor the conference room door. I, or anyone, could have been carrying a bomb. It was as though Kofi Annan, this man of peace, emitted an energy of peace greater than that attained by security personnel and technology.

As the Secretary-General spoke of the need for humanitarian care in Africa, Dr. Emoto's message about love and healing became clearer, and I realized we can learn much from people like Kofi Annan, Masaru Emoto, and John McConnell. We can learn that understanding and strength comes through the pursuit of peace.

Thank You & Tips

Thank you for joining me on my amazing adventures. I hope you've enjoyed our exciting experiences.

Here's a few tips I've picked up along the way.

I like a backpack rather than a suitcase. Weight travels better on shoulders than in hands, and a backpack leaves your hands free to carry temporary items or help others.

If you fly, slide your pack into a zippered sleeve to keep straps out of conveyor belts. Latch the zipper with a carabineer but not a lock.

Remember that you are an ambassador of your culture and a guest in another. Be kind, respectful, courteous. If you make judgments, keep silent.

Know that, even if you are of moderate economic means, you will be viewed as wealthy in many other countries. Fit in with local norms.

Smile. Your glowing countenance and genuine concern for your international brothers and sisters will open many doors.

Realize that you are an ambassador of peace. Your peaceful presence, even as an individual, speaks volumes about positive international relationships.

Consider taking: a partial role of toilet paper sealed in a plastic 18-ounce peanut butter jar with a screw lid, extra carabineers and straps on your pack, a few spring-clip clothespins, mentholated topical cream, petroleum jelly, talcum powder, cough drops, first aid kit, Ace bandage, sewing needles, tweezers, sturdy toothpicks, bandanas, sleep mask, headlamp, electrical adapter, spare batteries, something lightweight to give away (postcards of Michigan are great to show where you live).

Author's Bio and Books

Robert M (Bob) Weir was born in Port Huron, Michigan, USA, on February 22, 1948, and was raised in his family's farm implement business in the nearby village of Emmett.

He graduated from Port Huron Catholic High School in 1966, Port Huron Junior College in 1968, and Western Michigan University in Kalamazoo, Michigan, in 1970 with a Bachelor's Degree in Communication Arts. He has a self-decreed PhD in Life.

Robert's career is in communications. He worked in radio, television, the school yearbook industry, and as a freelance writer and book editor.

He has authored 28 books, contributed to two by other authors, and written over 200 published articles. He has made dozens of presentations, speaking primarily about people, peace, social justice, travel/adventure, and the environment.

As a contract writer for business and industry, he developed and delivered more than two dozen training courses in the realm of management skills and technology.

Robert also served as a consultant and book editor for both established and emerging authors whose topics are primarily in the nonfiction realm of holistic health, metaphysics, human relations, and spirituality.

Reach Robert through his web site: www.RobertMWeir.com

Cobble Creek, short stories and poetry

Peace, Justice, Care of Earth: The Vision of John McConnell, Founder of Earth Day, biography

Dad, a diary of caring and questioning, parental care memoir

Brain Tumor: Life · Love · Lessons, medical memoir

Conversations through the Veil: Wisdom of the Spirits to Improve Our Lives, spiritual enhancement

Journey ... People, Places, & Ponderings,
series of 23 books on travel, adventure, and philosophy

- *Michigan Adventures, 1980s to 2000s*
- *Great Lakes Sailing, 1990s to 2003*
- *A Merry Time in Maritime England, August 2001*
- *Barbados, TransAtlantic, Spain, April & May 2010*
- *Greece, Bulgaria, Historical Seas Regatta, May & June 2010*
- *Germany: Kassel, Berlin, Hamburg, June 2010*
- *Russia: St. Petersburg, Pushkin, Moscow, June 2010*
- *India: Delhi, The Taj Mahal, July 2010*
- *India: The Himalayas, July 2010*
- *India: Ladakh, July 2010*
- *India: The High Ultramarathon, July 2010*
- *Hawaii & The Philippines, July 2011*
- *India: Delhi, Ladakh & The "Road" Between, August 2011*
- *India: Leh, Manali, Rewalsar, August 2011*
- *USA: Kalachakra; India: Dalai Lama, July & September 2011*
- *India: Pathankot, Amritsar, Delhi, Bodh Gaya, September 2011*
- *India: Kolkata, 2011-2012, 2014-2015*
- *India: Kolkatan Candle Lighters, 2012 & 2015*
- *Australia: Sydney, Gold Coast, Cape Tribulation, Tasmania, Winter Holidays 2013 & 2014*
- *Ecuador, Switzerland, Nepal, Caribbean Cruise, 2016, 2017, 2019*
- *USA: Road Trips, 2011 into 2021*
- *USA, South: Living Legacy Pilgrimage, Civil Rights Movement, November 2016*
- *USA, Four Corners, Fall 2021 to Spring 2022*

Outstanding People and Their Amazing Accomplishments

Reclaiming Lives: Rediscovering Myself While Educating Kolkata's Poor by Rosalie Giffoniello with Robert M Weir

MaxAbility: Who Are You? What Are You Here For? by Jeanne Hess with Robert M Weir

Made in the USA
Monee, IL
29 May 2023

34890597R00044